A

by the same author

Simple Men
Trust

Amateur

HAL HARTLEY

faber and faber
LONDON · BOSTON

First published in 1994
by Faber and Faber Limited
3 Queen Square London WC1N 3AU

Typeset by Wilmaset Ltd, Birkenhead, Wirral
Printed in England by Clays Ltd, St Ives plc

A CIP record for this book
is available from the British Library

ISBN 0-571-17213-X

2 4 6 8 10 9 7 5 3 1

Contents

1   Hal Hartley (photo by Richard Sylvarnes)

Introduction

Hal Hartley's *Amateur* is both a continuation and a departure for
the New York-based film-maker. Like his three previous
features, it is the story of a troubled man and a woman who
meet and edge towards a relationship, but who are restrained by
their circumstances and their self-doubts. The rhythm, the
ambience, and the *mise-en-scène* of *Amateur* are transparently the
work of the same precision engineer who made *The Unbelievable
Truth* (1989), *Trust* (1990), and *Simple Men* (1992). The irony,
the romantic negotiations, and the firmly-stoppered volcano of
emotions that identify Hartley's cinema can each be checked off
in this latest work: all present and correct.

Yet *Amateur* is Hartley's darkest film yet, a tragedy rather
than a melodrama. Its protagonists, the amnesiac pornographer
Thomas (Martin Donovan); Isabelle (Isabelle Huppert), the ex-
nun who falls in love with him; Sofia (Elina Lowensohn), his
young porn star wife, who has tried to kill him; and Edward,
the ex-crime accountant who tries to protect Sofia, are,
respectively, saturnine, melancholy, bitter, and cynical. We
have seen similarly disposed characters in Hartley's films before.
But where *Amateur* differs from its predecessors is in its
occupation of the thriller genre. The word 'occupation' strikes
me as particulary apposite, for while Hartley was never likely to
have churned out the kind of glossy sex-and-crime drama that
has become an atrophied Hollywood formula in the last decade,
its conventions and vernacular provided him with well-trodden
territory in which to explore his own preoccupations and, to use
an expression he uses a lot, 'do damage' to them. The title of
the film, I hazard, refers equally to Hartley the thriller director
as it does to Thomas or Isabelle, each of whom is tentatively
making his or her way in a new world.

The premise – a Hal Hartley action thriller, or romantic
thriller – is instantaneously incongruous. We are not used to
hearing people in his films talk about 'high-level government
corruption' or such entities as the 'highly respectable yet

ultimately sinister international corporation with political connections' from which Thomas, Sofia, and Edward have fled. Hartley, in fact, italicizes this kind of thrillerspeak in the dialogue, drawing attention to its generic function and to its absurdity. There is in the film a kindred fascination with the jargon of business and modern consumer technology. When Sofia asks Edward about some incriminating 'floppy disks' (which, as she and later Thomas observe, are neither 'floppy' nor 'disks') and tells him that she intends to be 'a mover and a shaker', Elina Lowensohn's brilliant line readings convey all the amateurism of someone using these phrases for the first time, discovering them as found objects. This deliberate self-consciousness lays bare the way we appropriate and reinvent language and rob it of its original meanings.

Amateur, then, is not simply a film that's about what it's about. The intellectual enquiry here extends to analyses of – or, at least, a worrying about – the sexual objectification of women and movie violence. Because Thomas, desocialized by amnesia, and Isabelle, reborn into a secular existence, are innocents abroad, they are the perfect guinea-pigs with whom to confront such potentially alienating influences as pornography and 'sexy clothes'. (A line spoken by Isabelle, 'I know nothing about sex, perversion or violent crime,' was cut from the film as if it spelled out too plainly the philosophical quest behind it.) Hartley, though, does not proselytize; where *Simple Men* quietly concluded that misogyny is self-defeating, *Amateur* is more concerned with examining than pontificating about the sexual dynamics between men and women. Accordingly, in his presentation of violence – a slapstick violence as choreographed as the dance sequences in *Simple Men* and Hartley's TV film *Surviving Desire* (1991) – Hartley sets up torture and shootings as something he is testing, not something he is indulging for his or our pleasure. In all these respects, *Amateur* is his most political film so far, and his least comforting.

The following interview took place in Hartley's Greenwich Village apartment on 21 February 1994. It was the fourth time we had sat down with a tape recorder in front of us in two years; I had originally interviewed him for Faber's 1992 book of the *Trust* and *Simple Men* screenplays. Affable but exceedingly modest and softly spoken, Hartley talks both methodically and passionately about his films. Their visual and verbal economy, and the impression they give you of being made the only way they could have been made, is reflected in their maker's meticulousness and his general disdain for the extraneous. There is no fat here at all: Hartley's mien is as lean as his aesthetic (even his name is tidily alliterative).

So the movies become the man – in this case, a singular, driven *auteur* of modern manners striving to make order of emotional turmoil by rigorously distilling it into images of fervid purity. But a word of caution: *Amateur*, like Hartley's other films, has a big heart. Among several peripheral characters who encounter the central quartet is Officer Patsy Melville, a policewoman so scandalized by the random cruelty of the world that she shows an endearing solicitude to each casualty or criminal who fetches up at the precinct where she is on booking duty. It's a piece of characterization and a performance, by actor Pamela Stewart, that 'does damage' to our expectations about thrillers and cops and the very notion of screen drama in the most delightful and Hartleyesque way.

Graham Fuller
June 1994

'Being an Amateur'

GRAHAM FULLER: *Reading the diary notes that you kept before and during the making of* Amateur, *I got the sense that, without wishing to step too far away from your previous experience as a film-maker, you were trying to strip away as many preconceptions as possible. This is reflected in the film itself, which is the story of a man, Thomas, who has lost his memory; a woman, Isabelle, who has left a nunnery and become a novice in the world; and another woman, Sofia, who is also trying to reinvent herself but represents the past that will eventually catch up with Thomas. Then, in terms of yourself, you wrote of an urgency to 'look for images more than construct them, find them rather than invent them'. Indeed, your earliest diary entry says, 'I need to see better. So much of the time I feel my looking is poisoned by convention. Why is it that when I'm shooting, I miss so much, I don't leave myself open?'*

Tell me how the 'amateur' status of the characters in the film, each of whom is in the process of being reborn, meshes with your own need, especially your need on this particular film, to rethink your approach as a maker of images.

HAL HARTLEY: I guess the initial idea was that by having characters who were completely fresh and, on some level, uninformed, I would be provided with an excellent narrative vehicle in which *I* could look at things fresh. On one level, the film was meant to be an exercise in discarding habits.

One of the things I find perhaps a little troubling is that the only thing I did manage to look at fresh and rediscover in its fundamental essence was narrative film-making convention. I don't know if I managed to achieve a seriously fresh view of the world and my experience of it, outside of being a film-maker.

A lot of that has got to do with fear. Despite my earliest inclinations, through the evolution of the film I felt an increasing need to adhere to narrative conventions. The more I pressed against the envelope of those conventions, the more I feared the film wouldn't appeal to anyone on any level.

Nevertheless, right up till the end, there's been this strong urge to just say, 'To hell with it. Don't worry about the audience. Don't worry about the people. Your job is to look.

Your vocation is to look, not to entertain. Entertaining comes second. You should consider yourself somebody who can be entertaining by virtue of the sincerity and the rigorousness of his ability to look.'

I don't think I got there. I don't even know if I wanted to get there. I like telling stories. I'm just always concerned that I could be telling stories that are somehow more immediate if I reassess my use of the tools.

GF: *Did you feel that you at least got* close *to your stated intent?*

HH: There are moments. Like in any of the films, there are things I think succeed and things I think fail. But the character of these individual successes and failures are subsumed by the more general character of the entire film. They all become part of this film, which, through being constructed, discovers and maintains its own integrity. And that means, usually, story. This is a piece of fiction, after all is said and done. If it seems that the storyteller is not trying to get away with something which he hasn't earned, then you feel entertained.

I'd have to think about specific examples of what worked. I think that image of Thomas sitting up in the street at the beginning is a success. Also Thomas sitting down with his back to us toward the end and giving that speech. It's funny to use the word 'success' in regard to yourself. But what I mean is that I really had to fight to get that image of him with his back to us. I had to fight to see it. I had gotten it wrong the first time we shot it. I had shot that scene in an entirely different way – much more elaborate, even theatrical. Thomas was walking away from the camera as it dollied behind him, stopping every few feet and looking back over his shoulder to speak to Isabelle. It was still pretty much about Thomas's back. The back of his head. About being deprived of seeing the actor's face. But I hadn't gone far enough. Then, by looking at the footage of that first attempt, I did discover what I needed to go out and try to see. Just discovering the energy of looking at someone's back, was, I felt a success.

GF: *Was that shot an instance of something that happened on the day, or had you thought about it before?*

HH: I hadn't really thought about it. I mean, I've got notes. A lot of those concerns originated in my notebook, which goes all the way back to 1987. For example (*reads*), 'The back of someone's head is part of that person, too, worthy and necessary to be seen.' Discoveries of this nature are the result of admitting your vulnerability at the moment of shooting. I need to let myself be affected by the circumstances of shooting and respond in a direct way and avoid chickening out and settling for an approach that is a convention.

The things that contributed to those particular circumstances are interesting. We had an epidemic of hepatitis during the filming; another film shooting in New York did too. Well, Martin [Donovan, who played Thomas] got it right at the end of production. He was sick the day we reshot at the Cloisters [a monastic building in upper Manhattan], which was a pretty expensive thing to have to do, anyway. It was good for him to be sitting because he was physically weak. It was actually necessary to have him turned away from the camera because he looked sick.

GF: *You couldn't have used a body double?*

HH: No. We needed his movements, his gestures. At that point in the movie any attentive or even inattentive viewer would be so intimate with Martin that they would know if it wasn't him. I'm reassured by that shot now. It achieves the type of thing I think movies do best.

GF: *It's the kind of eloquent ellipsis that you use a lot in your films; you see the man but not his face. In an earlier scene, you have a close-up of Edward's feet while he's being tortured with electricity. It's a way of giving information that somehow intensifies the emotions.*

HH: Yes, in detail. A lot of the situations in this movie strike me as standard TV cop show stuff, but with the information changed. A TV cop show made by someone who doesn't know how to make TV cop shows. Again, it seems to me that what I managed to do here, if anything, is look at movie conventions from a more individual perspective.

GF: *Did the fact that you were working within a specific genre – the romantic thriller – heighten your need to break away or somehow alter the tropes of that genre?*

HH: It heightened my need to reassess how I was going to achieve a standard genre device. I would look at the script, the space, the actors, and say, 'How am I going to do this in some way that interests me?' I wanted to avoid making *Amateur* an exercise in genre. But I found myself feeling I was making a genre film. The script is kind of written that way.

2 Martin Donovan

3   Hartley with Huppert and Martin Donovan's back

GF: *Amateur is clearly recognizable as one of your films. Not just
because of the presence of familiar faces like Martin Donovan,
Elina Lowensohn, and Damian Young; in texture, tone, style, and
structure, it's of a piece with* The Unbelievable Truth, Trust, *and*
Simple Men, *albeit darker. It's patently not a* thriller *thriller, if
you take my meaning.*

HH: Yes.

GF: *It prompts the question, have you seen a lot of modern
Hollywood thrillers?*

HH: Not really. My cinematographer Michael Spiller and I went
to see some John Woo movies. We saw *Jurassic Park*, too: that
scene when the car is falling down through the tree on top of
the pseudo dad and kid was great. Nobody does that stuff better
than Steven Spielberg. We watched those types of things.
Action, suspense. I saw *The Fugitive*. But I realized that what I
liked about the action in that film was that they were ready and
willing to have a real train crash. That was exciting, but worlds
away from the reality of my situation.

4 Hartley and cinematographer Michael Spiller in discussion . . .

5 . . . on the set

No matter what I was watching, I realized that suspense is built around doors and obstacles. I've been telling myself this for years. Even comic suspense tends to be about someone wanting something and having something else in their way. Then I go to see *Jurassic Park* and they tell you right off the bat that these dinosaurs can open doors.

GF: *You used that farceur's trick of having characters coming and going through doors, looking for each other, in* The Unbelievable Truth, Simple Men, *and you do it here again in* Amateur.

HH: Yes. I've built a hide-and-seek scene into all of the films. It's no longer there in *Trust*, though. That one didn't work so well. It was supposed to be complicated and funny, but turned out to be simply confusing. The one in *Simple Men* with Dennis chasing Elina around Kate's apartment was my favourite thus far. In *Amateur*, it realizes itself in the scene where Edward scopes out the country house. Like I said in the notes, this is the logical extension of suspense in the direction of the dangerous.

GF: *What do you mean?*

HH: I've found that this notion of suspense is integral to telling stories, even if you're not making a conventional suspense movie. It's about showing the audience just enough of a situation so that they can have fairly clear expectations, and then you think of ways of thwarting those expectations and surprising them. My earlier films, which I see as melodramas, were all constructed this way. *Amateur*, which I think of as a tragedy, does this, too, but instead of the surprise being funny, it's meant to hurt. This manipulation of expectation is, I guess, much more clearly described in discussions of Hitchcock.

GF: *Certainly you've played with suspense before. While you were talking, I had a flash back to the climactic scene in* Trust, *when Matthew is threatening to blow up the factory with a hand-grenade.*

HH: Right. And in a more mysterious, less concrete way in *Simple Men*, where an atmosphere of romance and intrigue is generated through suspicion and vulnerability. In *Amateur*, I wanted concrete activity. I found myself cutting out a lot of dialogue. Things just didn't need to be said. The images said a lot on their own.

GF: *Going back to this notion of your needing to cut away your*

preconceptions, did you feel that you had imposed too many of them
on the other films and that you wanted to free yourself up? You have
often spoken of this idea of being able 'to do damage'.

HH: Radical reassessment. What I think a scene is supposed to
be about doesn't matter once I begin editing. Whatever I
thought of, or expected from, these images before they became
a reality is irrelevant. I always forget this and have to go
through the agony of relearning it. It's about doing damage to
my preconceptions. I have to look at things for what they are
and distinguish this from what I *think* they are.

GF: *But had you felt that you'd imposed too much on the other*
movies?

HH: No. But sometimes I feel tired of subordinating any kind of
creative impulse to the laws of dramatic verisimilitude; to telling
a story so that it seems like real life. I have loved doing fiction,
but the urge to move away from fiction film-making is quite
strong in me now. I want to do other things a lot of the time.
Maybe it's just a phase I'm going through, but I want to shake
it up again. I need it to be shook up.

GF: *June 1993 seems to have been a critical month for* Amateur.
The so-called 'ultimate' version of the script was dated June 4. Then
there were some amendments before the final draft, dated June 18.

HH: Yes, that was the one we took out to shoot.

GF: *On June 9, you speak in your diary about the 'fragmentary*
nature' of your script for the short film, The Heart Is a Muscle. *Did*
that script and the Amateur *script evolve at the same time?*

HH: The first draft of *Amateur* was written simultaneously with
The Heart Is a Muscle. I felt a lot more free with *Heart* because
it wasn't a script I knew I was already slated to make. I wrote
Amateur knowing that Isabelle Huppert was going to do it and
that there was already something of a schedule to keep in mind.
There was all this attention and expectation right from the start
that made me feel a little pressured to provide something, if not
popular, at least a bit more accessible – although the script of
Amateur may, in fact, be a bit more radical in its narrative
techniques than the film itself. Originally, I had Isabelle
narrating the scenes she was in as if she were the omniscient
author. I thought it might bring the artifice of the storytelling
right up to the surface in a way that also functioned within the
purely fictional context of the story. But it wasn't dynamic or

interesting. I didn't pull it off. Isabelle Huppert and I worked hard on it, too. I'm still interested in that device, though, and I think I'll try it again in a smaller, workshop-type project.

GF: *Did writing* The Heart Is a Muscle *influence what you would do in* Amateur?

HH: The character of Muriel in *The Heart Is a Muscle* came to life in an afternoon, out of the blue, and I was fascinated by her. I really fell in love with this person. Although there are big differences between Muriel and Isabelle in *Amateur*, I essentially began forming Isabelle out of this young girl in the other script. For a start, both are virgins who want to lose their virginity.

GF: The Heart is a Muscle *is a much lighter script and funnier on the page than* Amateur, *although it also ends with a death.*

HH: I think I manage to stay outside the minds of the characters in *The Heart Is a Muscle* and just look, conscientiously, at the outsides of their hearts. I was rereading the collected writings of Brecht during that summer. A lot of that script is basically exercises in things Brechtian. I took Brecht's 'traffic accident'[1] example and put it wholesale into *The Heart Is a Muscle*. Near the end there's a truck driver who has accidentally killed Muriel. Although clearly distraught, he simply describes what happened and adds a brief note about his emotional state. I find this kind of gesture very moving, very compelling.

GF: *In* The Heart Is a Muscle, *as in all your films, you have*

---

[1] Hartley is referring to the essay *The Street Scene: A Basic Model For An Epic Theatre*, by Bertolt Brecht.

'It is comparatively easy to set up a basic model for epic theatre. For practical experiments I usually picked as my example of completely simple, "natural" epic theatre an incident such as can be seen on any street corner: an eyewitness demonstrating to a collection of people how a traffic accident took place. The bystanders may not have observed what happened, or they may simply not agree with him, may "see things a different way"; the point is that the demonstrator acts the behaviour of the driver or victim or both in such a way that the bystanders are able to form an opinion about the accident.'

Then, a page later:

'If the scene in the theatre follows the street scene in this respect then the theatre will stop pretending not to be theatre, just as the street corner demonstration admits it is a demonstration (and does not pretend to be the actual event).'

(*Brecht On Theatre*. Translated by John Willett)

characters stating what's uppermost in their minds, which goes
against the grain of most film dialogue. Here, you have Dave coming
right out and saying, 'Sarah, marry me.' Mike says it to Pearl in
The Unbelievable Truth, *Jude to Katie and Katie to every passer-*
by in Surviving Desire . . .

HH: Matthew asks Maria to marry him in *Trust*, too. And in
Theory of Achievement, the Bob Gosse character proposes to
Ingrid. Obviously, it's a big thing in my mind, huh? Well, you
know, it just seems to me to be one of those things people say.

GF: *But isn't that kind of emotional candor something that people are*
often too frightened or inhibited to reveal?

HH: In real life?

GF: *Yes.*

HH: I guess so. Taking things we say by rote, that are habits, or
knee-jerk reactions, and putting them in a context where they
have to be understood literally – that's actually a good example
of a technique I use. A mode of expression I return to often.

GF: *Thomas, in* Amateur, *is also a film-maker – a pornographer, in*
fact. Do you think that his amnesia represents an unconscious wish
on your part to free yourself from something?

HH: It was not unconscious – it was totally conscious. The only
thing I could make a movie about at that time was a man who
wanted to escape his responsibilities. I wasn't feeling guilty
about anything in particular, but I was afraid I had made a lot
of mistakes both in my personal life and my work life.

My company, True Fiction Pictures, had become an
enormous responsibility, and there was this realization that I
either had to let it grow and generate more responsibility for
myself or stop it altogether. It's as though a business venture
has a life of its own and it has to be fed. You could starve it to
death, too, I suppose. But that didn't seem to be an option.

I did *not* want to be a businessman. And I did not want to
drift into a situation where I'd have to do work I didn't love
simply to pay the bills. I felt like I was being carried away from
myself as a result of being relatively successful.

Making Thomas a film producer evolved out of this. As for
his connections to these criminals, I had no understanding of
the crime world. But I understood something about business
and I realized that business and crime often look very similar.
When I was at Cannes with *Simple Men* in 1992 some people

were explaining to me about the Triads, gun-running out of Israel and other parts of the Middle East, and how capital from this kind of activity gets funnelled into pornography and other film-related businesses – I was fascinated. It was the only time I became interested in crime, and I believe it was by virtue of its resemblance to business-as-usual in my own field. The story I ended up writing seemed to function as a neat example of how ferocious crime can trickle down into our more mundane experiences.

GF: *Do you feel you used the crime strand of* Amateur *as a kind of MacGuffin to facilitate the relationship between Thomas and Isabelle?*

HH: I needed her to meet a man who is really quite good and honest, but whose past – the past he can't remember – is mean and dangerous. I needed a situation that begged the question: does culpability vanish just because someone changes their ways? You can witness this story from either Isabelle's or Thomas's point of view. You can see it as the manifestation of a miracle or as a sort of blueprint for a coincidence. I wanted to construct and perform a single story that provided both points of view with everything they needed to argue their case within the film. I'm interested in our distinctions between miracles and coincidences.

GF: *Were you able to preserve the integrity of both the miraculous and the non-miraculous in telling the story?*

HH: Yes, definitely, although it's a subjective thing in the end. I've found myself not caring whether it's a miracle or a coincidence. What's the difference?

GF: *Going back to the diary, it seemed you occasionally lost sight of your intentions – or felt that you had. You wrote on May 23, 'I keep grazing the edges of inspiration as regards* Amateur. *I'm not obsessed.' Was there a point when you did become obsessed with the film?*

HH: I don't think I did. And I question whether I've ever been obsessed with the movies. My movies. There's complete immersion. Inspiration – I think I got that. The thing is to try and fashion formal conceits out of ideas and feelings you really care about and are interested in. I think that when I wanted obsession I was simply anxious for my life to seep into the work. There are stages, naturally, when the work is mostly just the formal conceits: intellectually understood, skilfully crafted perhaps, but still waiting to be inspired. And that takes time and crisis.

In the editing stage, I rediscovered total immersion. I often have to reach a moment of crisis before I really start looking at things fresh. When you're in a crisis situation you can't afford to take things for granted. You're forced into an immediacy you don't experience every day. For example, I found I'd shot this film in a much more radical way than I thought I had. But when I was shooting it, I was walking away from the set each day, saying, 'I'm just a hack!'

GF: *What radicalism was there?*

HH: I built the images so that it was very difficult to make normal, narratively continuous scenes. I remember yelling at the wardrobe girls a lot: 'Don't mess with his tie!' 'But, Hal, in the other shot he was . . .' 'Don't mess with his tie! Everything's fine the way it is right now!' And, you know, not only was the actor's tie different, but so was his chair, and he was in a totally different position. So I was indifferent to continuity. Continuity bugged me. It got in the way of the image. When it came to editing these images, I was forced to reconsider the necessity of seamlessness and continuity on a moment-to-moment basis. The way I shot the picture pretty much determined that I would *have* to have ellipses, I would have to have jump cuts.

GF: *You also changed the order of certain scenes within the story structure. For example, the scene where Sofia drives off from Grand Central Station is followed by the scene between Isabelle and the magazine editor, George, talking about the pornographic story she's written, instead of the scene between Kurt, Jan, and Edward, which followed it in the script. Also the scene where Jan and Kurt are menacing Sofia is interrupted by a scene between Edward and sympathetic Officer Patsy at the police precinct. What's interesting about this is that each of those scenes is a discrete entity, and that you were able to shuffle the deck a little bit to streamline the narrative.*

HH: Yeah. Thank God, because if I couldn't I'd have really been screwed.

GF: *Do you think this would be possible in a Hollywood film?*

HH: I think that's one of the things that probably does happen a lot in more conventional films. The script often promises something quite specific: a certain tone, a particular sense of intrigue perhaps. But the translation of words on a page to moving pictures is an enormous leap. The completed images, made up of the actors' personalities and the cinematographer's instincts and sensitivity, deliver an entirely new, concrete rhythm and pace. That's the reality of the movie now, not the script. You start to say, 'Well, what would happen if I took scene seven and put it where scene three is now?'

GF: *In this case, you felt the need to accelerate the story?*

HH: Yes. Especially the middle section – reel three and the beginning of reel four. From the time Isabelle and Thomas go in to the loft until the moment they escape from it with Sofia was like a twenty-minute thing. We began saying, 'Man, we're in this loft forever. Why don't we break it up? And where is Edward? We've forgotten all about him.' So we cut in scenes of Edward grabbing the phone from the woman on the street and being arrested and then at the precinct. Once again, it's part and parcel of doing damage to your preconceptions about the film.

GF: *In your diary, you wrote, 'I've always believed that if there is a problem in the script, it will be there in the movie.' In retrospect, were there any problems in the* Amateur *script when you started shooting?*

HH: I have never gone out and shot a film thinking that there were holes in the script that I hoped to discover ways of filling when I got to the set. But I do leave myself open to the emergence of a better understanding. And then I have to believe, when I first set out, that things are going to change. The shooting script is proof that I understand everything I need to shoot in order to tell the story adequately. And in my case it has always been very well understood, so changes aren't enormous.

GF: *Knowing how precisely you work, and having read the script before I saw the completed film, I was very surprised by how much was cut, although at the same time there are long scenes that appear more or less word for word; there's one scene between Sofia and Edward in which just one or two words are changed. On other occasions, you've lopped off the entire endings of scenes. It reminded me of the way an editor on a daily newspaper will chop off the end of a story to make it fit, though presumably your reason for doing this was that you felt everything had been said in those scenes and that there was no need to linger.*

HH: In the later stages of editing, I discovered that so many of the scenes began, continued, and then ended, as if they had an arc – and that's not so good. A lot of times when you're trying to make a whole story that has an arc, to build it up with all these little arcs is a problem.

As far as cutting off the ends, it's about suspension. You don't want everything to be answered and sewn up at the end of each scene. You want to leave the end hanging, and then go on to another scene so that you can get back to the part that was left hanging later. It's also about momentum. The audience should always be falling forward, because there's a carrot being dangled in front of them – or whatever metaphor you want to use. Also, I think I just over-wrote, I repeated ideas, and those were places where cuts were necessary.

GF: *Was it also a case of cutting things that were tending to make explicit what had already been implied, particularly in the scenes between Thomas and Isabelle?*

HH: Yeah. I found that the images themselves often said a lot of things that the dialogue was written to say. That was a big step for me – to let the images do the talking and make people shut up.

GF: *What was the ratio between the scenes that you shot and then cut to those that were eliminated during rehearsal or on the day?*

HH: I think I shot everything that was written, and it was in the editing stage that I reduced or cut them. There are some scenes that were completely out that came back in toward the end. I took certain scenes out after I edited the film according to how it was written. I'd say, 'No, this one's too slow, and maybe this one isn't necessary' – so whole scenes went. I took the scene with George out. I took the scene with Thomas meeting the kid on the bench out in one of the early cuts. For two or three cuts they weren't in the movie. And then by moving things around, I discovered places where they would be appropriate and actually add to the information and improve the flow.

GF: *There were a few occasions where little bits of dialogue were added: for example, when Thomas is renting one of Sofia's porno videos in the video store and he talks to the long-haired assistant guy, a two-line exchange was added.*

HH: That was something that happened in casting, when Currie Graham, who ended up playing that role, came in to read. I had just seen twenty guys read that one-page scene with Martin. Currie came across as this personality. He gives a very funny, skewed emphasis to things that I found really different, and that gave really new meaning to the scene. It kind of implies a whole bunch of other, sick kind of things – which was not necessarily in the script.

GF: *When new things emerge in rehearsal – new words, new bits of dialogue – do you then write them into the script?*

HH: On occasion, if they really seem to work. That was a good example. But, for instance, the two actors, Parker Posey and Dwight Ewell, who play Nicola and Ted, the squatters who find Edward and bring him back to life, were almost incapable of settling down long enough to rehearse anything without throwing things in. They've been in smaller parts in other films of mine and they're very good friends, who joke around constantly, like two kids. And I really like that energy; I love working with them. I think the dialogue I wrote for them was probably culled from the two or three rehearsals we had.

GF: *Do you allow any dialogue improvisation on camera?*

HH: No. I prefer not to let that happen. Sometimes we get a particularly unruly actor who will do that kind of thing, and if it works, it works. On a film like this, I think I would just let it go, even if it blew the take. I wouldn't necessarily reprimand them. On this film I allowed myself to watch actors a lot more, to let the camera run. There were a lot more takes and there are a lot more shots in this movie that are 'full shots', where the actors are all head to toe in the same frame, and they move around within the frame without me cutting. I cast Dwight and Parker particularly for those kind of quirky, moment-by-moment reactions that they have. You don't want to clip that too much. You want to give it some structure and see what they can do.

I guess that's a level of improvisation. I think that's happening more as time goes by and I make more films. You may not deviate from the script or even from the way you want the actors to move around the room, but that still leaves you open to a huge amount of possibility. I think I've looked a lot for that in this film. When Edward and Sofia meet in the

Angelika café, in the scene where you first meet Edward, it's a two-shot; Edward is in the foreground, smoking, and Sophia is talking about how she pushed Thomas out the window. I remember thinking, 'Yeah, I don't want to impose on this; I don't want to cut.'

GF: *You repeated that set-up in the scene in the roadside diner when Thomas finally talks to Sofia.*

HH: Except this time Sofia is in the foreground.

GF: *Is that a deliberate symmetry?*

HH: I can't say that I was relating it to the first scene narratively, but it comes from the same place and from the same formal and aesthetic concerns. I was sitting in this place, trying to figure out how best to facilitate the scene. Once again I said to myself, 'Don't break this up. This is not something you want to edit into two single shots.' I'd learned a lot from a scene in *Surviving Desire*, which I'd liked on the page but not the way I'd shot it. It's a scene where Martin Donovan's character is talking to Mary Ward's in a bar, and I'd shot it in two singles. It had none of the life that it should have had, because I broke it up. It should have been a long-lens two-shot, allowing the actors to go out of focus if necessary. Breaking shots into singles can deprive a scene of its immediacy.

GF: *Each of those set-ups in* Amateur *is unconventional, because although there are obviously situations where people do converse that way, you very seldom see it in the movies. More often than not, you'll get single shots from one character to another, or a profile shot of them talking across a table.*

HH: I've noticed a lot of times that we don't always look at each other, and sometimes it's much more interesting to detail the way people avoid contact than it is to detail the way people try to gain contact.

GF: *What you're doing, in effect, is creating an image that spatially formalizes the emotional distance between characters, which, in the case of Thomas and Sofia, is integral to the story. It's a way of using composition to elaborate on what we already know about them from the story.*

HH: The characters' relationships to each other and to the audience are called into question, or emphasized and underlined. We see Sofia right up close. Her reaction to Thomas's pleas are not seen by Thomas; they're seen by us. But we can see both her and him, all in the same little, compact, uninterrupted chunk of time. That's something Tarkovsky constantly talks about in *Sculpting in Time*: the idea of not interrupting the film. I wasn't thinking about Tarkovsky when I was making this film, but I've been rereading that book and I think I know what he's talking about now. I think there is an immediacy there, a dramatic pitch that's achieved that would not have been achieved if the dynamics within those shots had been changed.

GF: *Do you think it's a form of deconstruction?*

HH: Well, it's reassessment. I just read an article in *The New York Times* that made me think that all my life I've been using the term 'deconstruction' the wrong way.

To me it's just been the simple thing of deconstructing something, taking your toy apart and seeing how it works and putting it back together and appreciating it in a different, more intimate way. So maybe that's what I'm doing.

GF: *Well, you've taken a conventional two-shot, analysed what it is, and put it back on the screen with the elements rearranged, and there's a tension in the image that wouldn't exist if you'd plonked the camera on them sitting opposite each other at the table.*

HH: It's about twisting it inside-out.

GF: *It goes back to that idea of fragmentation you talked about earlier.*

HH: These are the dynamics that make going to the movies interesting to me: our relationship to the characters on the screen and, by extension, their relationship to each other. A lot of other people might describe it the other way around. They would say, 'No. It's about the relationship of the characters to each other and only then, by extension, to us.' In this regard, I was fortified by reading Alain Bergala discussing Godard. He distinguishes between composition and attack in Godard's work. You can set up a composition, but look at it from a different way. I should read it to you. Bergala says, 'Most shots in most films only take concrete shape as the result of a series of deductions which both programs them and progressively diminishes opportunities for the visual along the way . . . The scene is deduced from its function in the script; the shot is deduced from its function in the scene; the composition is deduced from its function in the shot; and the attack is more often than not deduced from the readability of the composition.' He goes on to suggest that Godard takes advantage of the film-maker's ability to treat composition and attack separately.

This gave me some confidence when I was trying to reconsider my habitual relationship to the characters in my films.

GF: *With the Thomas – Sofia shot, you are almost but not quite breaking the fourth wall.*

HH: Well, it's adding a different dimension to our relationship to the characters. We're seeing all these expressions on Sofia's face that Thomas is not seeing. Even though they are the ones having that conversation and we are outside it, we are nevertheless having a conversation with her that Thomas is not part of. I think it's one of the best shots in the whole thing. Every time I look at that picture, I see something new. And this has a lot to do with Elina [Lowensohn, who plays Sofia]. There's some really deep level of commitment and ability, and just soul.

GF: *In a letter you wrote to Scott Meek [of Zenith Productions], which is included in your diary, you suggested that 'the way in which Edward's torture is dealt with will decide the tone of the film.' Were you aware of an emerging difference in tone between the scenes with Edward, where he goes berserk at the pizza shop and kills the policeman after being tortured by Kurt and Jan, and the Isabelle – Thomas scenes, which remain fairly contemplative?*

HH: Yeah, I was aware of this. But neither Scott nor I were afraid of those things in the script stage. They didn't appear to be anything but perfunctory, driving the story forward.

I shot the scene of Edward assaulting the woman at the telephone booth at Fifth Avenue and 19th Street twice. That was a big deal, with the traffic going, people screaming, twenty-five extras, and thousands of people watching. When I walked away that night, I said, 'I don't think this is going to fit into this film. It's a very good scene and these actors have worked their hearts out but I just don't know if it's going to fit.' So I reshot it a couple of weeks later in an entirely different way. And that stayed in the film for a while but then came out. And then the first one went right back in. I had a lot of second guessing of my work on this film. By the time this scene got back in, it was because I found myself liking those kind of . . . seizures, whether they fit comfortably into the film or not.

GF: *That particular scene is possibly the most surreal you've ever shot, particularly when the two masked kids firing water pistols show up. When I saw it, I asked myself why you did it. There's a craziness to it.*

HH: And that's what I like about it now. It's unexplained, but not inexplicable. Well, no, maybe I've got it wrong. Maybe it is inexplicable. You can't figure out how you got there and what's going on, but you know what it means. It's violent. Something slamming into the middle of something else. It provides you with some narrative information and then keeps going berserk. I like that.

I've always used the word 'surreal' to mean framing or positioning something so that you can't explain what's what. It makes me think of those photographs you take on the beach when you hold your hand up and your friend stands forty-five feet away and it looks like you have a little person standing on your hand. That's kind of surreal.

Going back to the scene, I'd shot it so there was a little bit more at the beginning with the kids running through the frame and their mother is on the phone screaming at her husband, saying that she's going to throw them under a subway train. But it just wasn't working.

GF: *Along with copious slaps and shoves in your films, you frequently have characters pushing plates or glasses off of tables. Why did you cut the scene when Thomas does that in the diner in* Amateur?

HH: We shot it, but it showed him giving into his frustration too early and I found that alarming. He shouldn't blow his top then. There was also this thing when Isabelle and Sofia go upstairs to go to sleep and he kicks some stuff around in the kitchen. I took that out, too. It was better to keep it down and save it all for that image of him holding the gun to his head. Ultimately, he doesn't *really* blow his top at all. The next morning the telephone is ringing, and Sofia is still refusing to tell him who he is.

GF: *You keep the pot boiling.*

HH: Yes.

GF: *Your films seem to occupy a space somewhere between naturalism and non-naturalism.*

HH: I might use different words, but only because naturalism is often used to mean such a wide variety of things that it's a bit misleading.

GF: *An example of non-naturalism is the scene in the park between Thomas and the schoolboy where they're discussing* The Odyssey *and the porno magazine. It's played completely deadpan, but there's a major twist in it because the schoolboy's played by an actress.*

HH: I wanted the scene to operate on a different level, and I didn't think I could get that with a young boy. So I hired a twenty-two-year-old actress, Adria Tennor, and got her hair cut.

GF: *A decision like that completely changes what's going on in the scene, which is a discussion of pornography and the objectification of women, because you have an unexpected female presence.*

HH: Yes. It points out something about the language that's being used and the very nature of the conversation that they're having. There wasn't any particular thing I wanted to point out, but I will say that when I was writing that language, I was laughing, saying, 'Oh, this is so funny.' But I had a little twinge of embarrassment when I thought about women friends reading it. I said, 'If I'm going to make this kind of gesture, I should go a little further with it.'

GF: *Did the character of Isabelle, an ex-nun who smokes, grow out of the smoking nun in* Simple Men?

HH: Probably the opposite. It had been lingering for a while. It started when I saw a photograph of Glenda Jackson doing a movie in which she played a nun [*Nasty Habits*, 1976]. There was this picture of her and this other actress dressed as a nun taking a cigarette break on the set. I always thought it was a really funny image.

GF: *Isabelle Huppert, the actress who plays Isabelle and whom you named the character after, is not only the first star you've worked with, but an icon of European cinema. In films like Chabrol's* Madame Bovary *[1991], Huppert has embodied Catholic guilt, and I sensed you were aware of that because you cast her as a Catholic who's very anxious to lapse, who is really keen to have sex for the first time. How much did casting her influence the look and flavour of the film?*

HH: Generally, the recognition of the actors for who they are and what they represent as actors definitely has something to do with all that. I didn't sit down and write the script until after I

6   Hartley with Elina Lowensohn, Isabelle Huppert . . .

7   . . . and Damian Young

had spoken with Isabelle and told her the story. She seemed interested. She said, 'Ah, I'd like to play a nymphomaniac ex-nun.' Her enthusiasm for that influenced how I conceived of images of her when I was writing the script.

Michael [Spiller] and I found it impossible to ignore the fact that we'd look through the camera at Isabelle and see a certain portion of the history of French cinema. That was a little disconcerting at first, until we just embraced it. We did a lot of tests with different film stocks, taking into consideration what we would be dressing her in and the look of her hair.

There were certain things I had in mind when I was writing. When Thomas first comes into the coffee shop, she looks over her right shoulder, and that's a gesture she has done a lot in her career. She did it in *Violette Nozière* [1978], she did it in *Loulou* [1979]. I said, 'Do it. Let's embrace that.'

In the same way, I am conscious now that when audiences come to see a Hal Hartley film with Martin Donovan, they can't wait for Martin to knock something off a table, or break something, or smoke. Luckily, Martin is intrigued by that, too, but at one time he was a little afraid of it. He would say that he didn't want to become a puppet. But I think I convinced him that he's not. Movie actors can have characters that expand beyond the borders of each film, and I find that very interesting.

GF: *Elina Lowensohn's mystique in this film is enhanced by having seen her in* Simple Men. *She emerges as something of an icon in* Amateur.

HH: She is literally that at one point, when you see Sofia's image freeze-framed on the television screen and Isabelle reaches out to touch it. Isabelle's intent in touching it could be read in the same way that a Russian peasant might reach out to touch an icon. There is a mystique about Elina that is brought into being, I think, by the fact that she has got a pretty heavy accent. She is from a part of the world that we always consider here in the West as having a lot of mystery about it. She grew up in the shadow of the Carpathian Mountains in Romania, and you can hear that in her voice and see it in her look.

With Elina in this film, I was very interested in contradictions. She is someone who's got a very dignified air. You know she's got a lot of integrity just by the way she moves and speaks or the way she concentrates when she looks at you.

At the same time, she is very humble and not embarrassed to admit her naïveté about certain things. And that can make her hysterically funny. Also, she is somebody who knows all about the pleasures of being watched, of letting herself be seen. That's clearly part of why she's an actress. She is one of the few actresses I know who admits that, but at the same time she's one of the least vain people I know.

I sensed all those contradictions in Elina when we made *Theory of Achievement* back in 1990. By the time we made *Simple Men*, I was aching to work with her more and to really do something with these contradictions. They are the kinds of contradictions that are found in one person or one character; if you abstract it a little bit more, you can say those contradictions reside in one simple gesture. And those are the kinds of gestures that you suddenly realize you can't paraphrase, that you can't explain by all the talking or all the critical analysis in the world. Working with an actor like this seems to me to be the surest way of creating gestures that really become good images, because they won't lose their potency, because they are mysterious. Now, you can see, given what *Amateur* is about, why Elina was really at the centre of the conception of the movie, because I was already thinking about the mystery and the iconography of somebody who has been in a certain kind of crisis and actually gets reduced, physically as well as metaphorically, to an image. Specifically, that freeze-framed porno video image of Sofia on TV is based on a photo of Bernini's beautiful statue *Ecstasy of St Teresa* in the Cornaro Chapel, Santa Maria della Vittoria, Rome.

St Teresa was a pretty complicated person. She had always been sickly as a girl and pretty obviously very sexual – although she never did anything about it. It can be argued that she turned herself into a psychotic because of that. By the time she was twenty-five or so she completely flipped out and almost died. To us now, it sounds a lot like psychosomatic illness, but to her it was clearly her soul struggling with her body. Which is to say, it was a religious passion. In any event, having been quite devout to begin with, she entered a convent. She could apparently get herself in a state of prayer so intense that it would last for days. The Inquisition guys came to investigate her and decide whether or not she was some kind of crank.

They decided that she really had extraordinary gifts of prayer and asked her to write down everything about herself. She had never really been educated, but she nevertheless wrote an amazing book in which she described her life, her love of God, and what happened to her when she prayed. A lot of people, including psychologists and sociologists, have studied this book, because there was no doubt that she was sincere. She wrote with a kind of specificity and objectivity that was peculiar considering she was describing the subjective state of prayer. She didn't want to write this book, *The Life*. The Inquisitors made her write it because they thought it would be useful to other people, to other nuns.

When I was shooting the pornographic video footage, I tried to get Elina into a pose similar to this image of St Teresa. Sofia, who is, I would guess, supposed to be getting taken from behind, winds up frozen in a posture we appropriated from Bernini: an image of St Teresa in an agony of love, of ecstatic communion with God. What the photo doesn't show, by the way, is that the statue includes a figure of Cupid aiming an arrow at St Teresa's breast.

All this has to do with Sofia being reduced to an image that Isabelle is searching for. Now, we use this a lot in our vernacular. We say, 'I'm looking for a sign,' or, 'Something is going to show up in my life and point me in the direction I'm supposed to go.' I just took that literally and applied it to Isabelle: someone literally looking for an image, a sign, something, to point her in a direction. She feels deeply that she is supposed to do something with her life, but she doesn't know what. It turns out that she is supposed to protect this girl, Sofia.

The idea was that when Isabelle sees the image of Sofia she recognizes it as the sign she has been waiting for. She doesn't recognize it as a coincidence. She recognizes it as an image not simply representing knowledge, but containing it. That's why she touches it that way.

Years ago, when I was in college, I remember reading a magazine article in which some scientist was discussing how culture, life, science, whatever, was – through the advent of computers – approaching a form of reality very much in common with the Middle Ages. Back then, he argued, the cross was not simply a symbol, it was 'The Cross', and its power

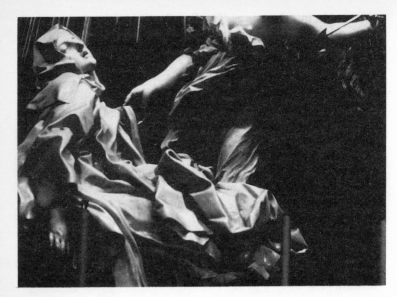

8   Bernini's Teresa . . .

9   and Hartley's

resided in its existence as 'The Cross': magic, in a certain sense. The article went on to say that computer chips don't convey information, they *are* information. The physical and the ephemeral become one. The seen and the unseen are connected again.

GF: *Sofia has had a brutalizing sexual life imposed upon her and has broken away from it, taking revenge on the man responsible; she intersects with Isabelle, who has abandoned a religious existence and is moving toward a sexual relationship with that same man. They almost exchange places.*

HH: I knew these two forces should meet. How and when they were going to collide was one of my major structural concerns during writing. In an earlier draft of the script it was implied that Sofia would stay in the convent where she and Isabelle and Thomas seek refuge – the same convent Isabelle has left. That implication isn't so strong now, but I still think it's significant she's in the convent at the end.

GF: *In terms of symbols and allegories – for example, in your use of the Sofia/St Teresa image – how much of the thinking behind that occurs before you sit down to write, or does it happen while you're writing?*

HH: I'm on the look out for it all the time. I'm trying to shoot a lot of video now. I want to do this project with Martin Donovan that a German company might give me money for. I said to Martin, 'Look, what we do is this: I just videotape you moving around smoking, walking, making gestures, or something like that. Then we'll put them into the computer and freeze-frame parts of them. Then we'll look at just these parts and try to isolate an emotional state that each of them makes us feel, and then start creating something from there.' I've always collected pictures and made collages that relate to the moving pictures I'm making. But it can go further.

To answer your question specifically, the St Teresa idea came in very early. Knowing what I knew about her helped me formulate the situation. Whether it was Isabelle's situation or Sofia's I wasn't sure.

GF: *The women in the film grow in strength, whereas Thomas has a much more desperate struggle defining himself in terms of women and sexuality. Edward, too, is uncomfortable when Sofia uses her sex appeal on him.*

HH: It seems to me that Edward has checked out on a lot of things. When we meet him in the movie, he's just somebody whose life has been so screwed up by his association with Thomas that it's hard for him even to be charmed by a woman. Eventually, the crust of all that comes off, and he thinks, 'What am I, an idiot? Sofia is a beautiful young woman, and I kind of like her, so I'm going to go to the country with her.' Unfortunately, things get in the way, but he manages before he goes crazy to do something quite heroic, which is refuse to tell Kurt and Jan where Sofia is.

Edward is this basically decent man who has become very cynical, but is ready to come back into the light of day and admit that people can be better. He doesn't really want to admit it when he meets Sofia at the café and almost makes fun of her when she says she's going to be 'a mover and a shaker'. By the time he's had a couple of martinis with her at Grand Central Station, he's willing to do a lot to protect her. Once he goes crazy, the same instincts make him irrational. By then, he'll do anything to save this girl, but it turns out tragically.

As for Thomas, he just wants to know who he is. He wants *help* in the beginning, although he doesn't remember the value of things, and he tends to be unprepossessing. Yet it seems to me that he discovers real ease in his new-found self with women. There's no stress at all for him in his relationship with Isabelle.

GF: *In one of your early notes about Thomas, you wrote: 'I don't want to dwell too much on his "I don't know myself". I'd rather emphasize his "I am someone new".' Do you feel that idea survived?*

HH: I think so. Initially, he wants to go to the police, but Isabelle asks him to stay the night. Then the next morning he again says he wants to go to the police because he had a scary dream about slicing somebody's face. And she's disappointed. It's like she doesn't want him to know who he was, whereas he thinks he might be dangerous to her. By the time he and Isabelle come across the razor blades and the Polaroid of a girl with her face cut up, he figures it's got to have something to do with him and he must have some idea who he is. He's very troubled when he walks into the next room and sees Isabelle dressed in this very sexy, frankly seductive clothing. He wants to get away from it. Martin and I talked about it as the first time

Thomas feels guilt even though he still can't remember what for. It's like when Adam and Eve did what they were always going to do and discovered they should be ashamed of themselves, basically for recognizing that you can have impure thoughts. Thomas felt tainted. He didn't want to touch Isabelle then.

GF: *But they do start to make love, don't they?*

HH: Only because she reiterates her belief in him. I think he's scared. And this is like the third time she says, 'I'm with you now. It doesn't matter to me who you were.'

GF: *Once again, you refuse to show sexual consummation. In fact, this movie, even more than your others, is agonized in that respect. Isabelle keeps asking Thomas to make love to her, but they never do. Even when they start to, you pan away.*

HH: He kisses her mouth, he kisses her shoulder, and then he begins to move down her body while the camera passes her. Michael asked me if we should be on Thomas and Isabelle kissing and then pan away. I said, 'No.' The movement has got to exist before the activity begins, so it can't be construed as looking away. It's not that I'm looking away – it's just that I've got my own trajectory. I'm looking at certain things. Martin Donovan and Isabelle Huppert happen to be in the shot for part of it. But the shot itself has its own determination.

GF: *Isabelle's desire to lose her virginity to Thomas is doomed. That lack of sexual resolution is disconcerting, a big part of the tragedy.*

HH: It's pretty sad – she doesn't get laid. But I think there's emotional resolution. As for the sex thing, I asked myself, 'What will give a sense of Isabelle's awakening sexuality more? Having a scene with her and Thomas making love, or them beginning to make love and step by step being introduced to new sensations and, of course, being interrupted. I think the interruption is necessary suspense. It holds out the opportunity that they'll go further later.

GF: *Like each of your other movies,* Amateur *is one prolonged coitus interruptus.*

HH: It's the principle of the striptease. Don't give everything away. If that part of Isabelle's quest had been achieved, it would have removed a large part of her struggle and most of the story: the testing of her hopes for Thomas. Isabelle [Huppert] understood her character's arc as wanting to be sensual, wanting to have these experiences, but being afraid of them as well. It was very important for her to approach it that way, because it made sense of her hesitation, particularly in the second half of the film, where her allegiance to Thomas is really tested by some of the things Sofia tells her about him. I was also conscious of the fact that Isabelle had made some pretty explicit movies in the past.

GF: *Much of* Amateur *was shot in medium close-ups, but you filmed the scene where Ted and Nicola find Edward in the squat in long shot. Why did you make that shift?*

HH: It echoed the shot when Jan and Kurt bring Edward into that space; they come in frame left and throw him against the wall. I just wanted to do the same thing with Ted and Nicola, make it recognizable. I simply liked the idea of people walking into shot talking. There was no real need to emphasize anything more than anything else.

The shot when Ted and Nicola are on the ground and giving Edward the scotch had a little bit more to do with the spontaneity of the actors when they were working together. And the third part of that is a two-shot of Ted and Nicola because there were specific things I wanted to emphasize in Edward's complete transformation to a gargoyle by having them looking at him. When you design a scene, you say, 'What is it that's really important here? What needs to be stressed?' And then you begin to figure out, 'Well, this should be a single, and then we should have reactions to it.' It comes down to stress.

GF: *You said in your notes that you wanted to find a new palette for* Amateur. *The palette you came up with was blacks and blues and wet street colours. Although you've never used bright colours, this is your darkest film. Was this dictated by the mood of the material?*

HH: Well, it could have been. I couldn't say it was for sure, though. A lot of the movie takes place at night and we were shooting in New York City and trying to build that palette out of what we saw around us – the kinds of bricks and cobblestones, the architecture, the wash on the buildings on lower Broadway. Some things we brought from *Simple Men*, such as the intense blue that we used in the night scenes. We were curious to see what that would be like in a city environment. When I look at this city, I see a lot of reflective surfaces – lights in the windows, glass, puddles – and that's really what I wanted to get at.

GF: *The palette on your Long Island films was drab, as befits the suburbs.*

HH: *Trust* was particularly grey; I remember we painted everything and added grey to all the paint to make it drab.

GF: *Did shooting a film in New York as opposed to Long Island or Texas* [Simple Men] *heighten the intensity of the experience?*

HH: In a very mundane way, because shooting and then coming home every night was a new experience. I'm used to living in hotels, and there is a whole different lifestyle that comes with that. You feel you've checked out of the normal way of living, and you can be consumed by the film. You live in the film.

On *Amateur*, I went home to my own apartment at the end of each day. It was hard to get used to. I wasn't sure if I really liked it. But on another level, I filmed things I saw all the time. It was very interesting to conceive of scenes and write them down at the script stage, knowing that they should take place at this deli or that coffee shop around the corner. I think that might be why, in a lot of the scenes, what happened could all be contained in one shot.

Otherwise, I don't think I would read much more into it than that. I was familiar with Long Island, too. Of course, there may be something about the character of New York and my relationship to it that informed my choices. There are a lot more angles in the city than Long Island, because there are so many more buildings. *Amateur* is different to *Simple Men*, which was conceived as a pastoral. When I think of *Simple Men*, I think of horizon lines.

GF: *Some of your angles in* Amateur *are almost Expressionistic.*

HH: Yeah, lots of acute angles. I thought a lot about Eisenstein and the geometric angles in his films, particularly when I knew I was messing with the spatial continuity in the scene between Thomas and Isabelle in the convent garden at the end. There are times when you want to feel the construction in a shot – the form the narrative has inevitably taken – and for no other reason than that I find it emotionally satisfying. The whole of that scene is a perfect example of a scene where I felt I had to keep my distance, in the Brechtian sense. I needed to display my method honestly and clearly, to involve the audience more, so that when Isabelle says, 'Will you make love to me?' there's a feeling of conclusion.

xxxix

GF: *The sequence of shots you use creates a kind of dissonance, so that the inevitability of his getting shot and the way you build up to it is far more interesting than the conventional suspense built around the premise that he could get shot and our hopes that he won't be. These moments in your films are less about pushing those kinds of buttons than they are an emotional examination of what's happening, and you harness your own formalism to that end.*

HH: I'm less interested in manipulating the audience's psychological and emotional connection to the characters than I am in really focusing their attention on the event of becoming interested in these actors playing these roles; I'm almost aspiring to have the audience moved by virtue of recognizing they're all in one big room with a strip of film passing through the projector.

It's like a laboratory experiment as well. I'm the scientist, perhaps, and I say, 'Witness – I am going to tell you everything in this movie, how it will end, what's going to happen, etc., and you're still going to be moved. You're going to become involved with these people even though you know this is all fake.' You see, to me, this capacity of fiction is a kind of miracle. But whatever it is, it resides in us. Human beings have the ability to let fiction do this to themselves. I also think that where this miracle works is in fiction that does not depend exclusively upon sentiment.

GF: *Although it does require us to suspend disbelief and our desire to consume something that makes us suspend disbelief.*

HH: That's why it works. It's absolutely our ability and willingness to suspend our disbelief that makes a more immediate contact between film and viewer possible, because it admits that people *want* to suspend their disbelief. Not admitting this ushers in cheap sentimentality: emotional effect as opposed to emotional involvement.

GF: *Why did you make Edward's slaying of Jan so comically protracted? It's virtually slapstick.*

HH: I became disgusted with myself for anticipating the excitement of gunplay on the set. During pre-production, we had a gun specialist and a man who was responsible for the 'squibs', which are these little packets of red paint with an electric charge embedded in them. You put one inside someone's shirt and when you hit the charge it looks like they've been hit by a bullet. We made a list of all the people who would be shot, saying things like, 'OK, this will be medium bloody, this will be very bloody, and this one will be medium-small bloody.' Stuff like that.

The first time a gun went off on set, I became immediately and deeply disgusted with guns, and I felt ridiculous having anticipated the excitement of making an image where it would have looked like someone really got shot. This interest in the realism of the gun shots was just so obviously foreign to the things I'm interested in that I was angry at myself. I don't generally have a problem with violence in movies, but then I don't spend much time around guns either.

The first shot we did that had a squib was when Thomas gets shot at the end of the movie. The sound of this gun made it more clear to me than anything else how cowardly a device guns are. From that point on, I just got an attitude about it and embraced my aversion to it. That aesthetic approach is something that has worked for me a lot in the past anyway. So I changed my attitude about the representation of hand-gun violence after that. I took it more seriously, more personally. By the time we were doing the shoot-out on the hill, Jan's death, I was at my most comfortable with the urge to work against . . . what? Standards, expectations, dramatic verisimilitude, whatever. My approach was to go *against*. In the end, I said, 'I've got two actors and a real gun with blanks. The actors will take care of the whole thing and who cares if it looks fake? Let's just see what impression the photography and the sound recording has on us. I'm willing to let it be as peculiar as possible.'

In the script it says, 'He shoots him again and again and again.' I knew it should be pathetic. But then I wanted it not only to be pathetic, but patently unreal, and then get pathetic despite the fact that it's patently unreal. Whether or not it seems unreal is unimportant; it's a disturbing gesture. I'm curious to see that scene with different audiences, to see if they laugh at the beginning or at the end of the shooting, or at all. I have a feeling people are gong to be freaked out by the end of the scene.

GF: *Jan keeps staggering on even though he's pumped full of bullets. I wondered if you were trying to kill off that overworked convention in movies of the last decade – including* Fatal Attraction *and*

Misery – where the seemingly dead villain keeps getting up to threaten the hero.

HH: I haven't seen those movies, but I did see *Cape Fear*, which was a similar kind of thing in that De Niro refuses to die. Michael and I had tried to see a lot of films where there was excessive gunplay action, and I am aware that there is a recent proliferation of quite good films that have serious violence. I think in *Amateur* I found my own personal voice in relation to that violence.

GF: *Do you think you were attempting to defetishize guns by what you did in that scene?*

HH: Again, I don't want it to seem like I had a very specific point to make in the way I handled certain things. But I would hope that the audience will become aware of me, my life, the actors' lives, and our work in making this film. I think that's why I kept the production recordings. All you hear during that shot, with the exception of some birds flying away at the start, is the recording we made while we did it. Besides the action, you hear the dolly being pushed along, and our feet moving along beside the dolly. It's the kind of thing you usually try to remove. But I came to recognize this whole shot as a response, a gesture of rebellion on my part, and I didn't want to water it down. It was my attitude at the time and it's part of the movie – as important as the dialogue.

GF: *Was it somehow disturbing to bring violence into the world of your movies for the first time?*

HH: Yes, it was disturbing, although not in the writing stage. Another aspect of trying to be as frank as possible for the audience, by being as fully engaged as possible, was that I had originally wanted the four lead actors – Isabelle, Martin, Elina, and Damian Young [who plays Edward] – to be called by their real names in the script. Everyone except Isabelle had a distinct problem with that, but I could understand that.

GF: *Tell me how you scored the movie.*

HH: I knew I wanted the score on this film to be bigger than on the others. On *Flirt*, my composing partner, Jeff Taylor, and I discovered some new musical things using cellos. We didn't use them because we only had synthetic strings to work with, but the music was starting to become, if not exactly orchestral, more of a band with horns and so on. By the time I finished *Flirt*, I

knew that *Amateur* was going to have a real cellist, a real
double-bass player, and a real violinist – a whole string section.
We holed up in this studio in Hoboken and did nothing but
watch the movie and play and yell and scream and play, and
after a few weeks, we had some eight hours of DAT recordings.
Then we got very serious. We moved into a new studio here in
New York and scored the whole movie to the videotape on our
keyboards. As someone who can't really play the piano, it was a
tremendous experience to go from writing the music on
keyboards to bringing in string players and two wonderful
singers. There were times when I wanted to quit and say, 'It
doesn't need to be this beautiful.'

GF: *The choral aspect of it, particularly at the beginning of the
movie, hints at the religious theme.*

HH: Yes, which is important because there's so little information
about that. There is also something very grand and tragic about
that first image of Sofia that made that music appropriate. It
definitely lets the audience know that bigger things are going to
be happening than this image of a man lying in a street.

GF: *What control will you exert in the marketing of the movie,
particularly since you've got some pretty sexy images of your actresses
that could be misused by an over-zealous distributor?*

HH: All that is a big distraction from being a film-maker. I used
to think that it was not only something I could contribute to,
but something that was right for me to be involved with. But
I'm getting more and more exhausted by having to deal with it,
particularly here in the States. Although, in retrospect, I think
Miramax did a good job with *The Unbelievable Truth*. They
went straight for the idea of putting a sexy image of Adrienne
Shelly on the poster. That's how you sell films, they said. I
questioned it because Adrienne and I were close at that time and
I had to live with her fear of being exploited. It was a concern of
mine, too, but it didn't hurt anybody – it helped. I think the
promotional materials for *Amateur* will probably utilize images
of the girls. I don't have a problem with it.

GF: *What about the effect it may have on audiences' preconceptions
about the film?*

HH: I'm not too worried. I think if they take any images from
this that appear, even out of context, to be much more explicitly
sexual than they are, it's OK. This movie doesn't shrink from

xliii

the representation of sexuality, and it has a very strong conscience about objectifying people – and women in particular. So, in that respect, it seems to me it almost can't go wrong.

GF: *What reservations, if any, do you have about presenting women as sex objects in your films?*

HH: My feelings are that I have never had any problems with objectifying women in the films. For instance, it was interesting to me that some feminists considered *Trust* a good film – and for feminist reasons. *Trust* is nothing but the conscientious construction of a pedestal on which to put the young woman of my dreams. It is absolutely the highest and most well-achieved and finely wrought piece of objectification I have ever done in my life. And I was so successful at it that I made *Simple Men* as a result – as if to say, 'Oh, man, what have I done?' Because I started to question my own motives after I finished it. The woman embodied by Adrienne in *Trust* just happens to be the kind of woman I like. It also just happened to be the kind of woman that a lot of feminists liked.

GF: *What about in* Amateur?

HH: I think they're the kind of women I like, too. I like beautiful women. They are always in my films, and I put them there. I think characters have to be dealt with respectfully, though. If I didn't find people inherently interesting, I wouldn't be interested in forming characters. And if I didn't find people inherently mysterious and intriguing, and by extension, sexually appealing, all my characters would be the same. I think it's important to try to draw characters who may be quite foreign to your own feelings, moral assumptions, and political or philosophical stance. So it was with some relief that I could have Sofia behaving as she does and photograph her wearing certain clothes and being overtly sexual. When we talked about Sofia, Elina and I agreed, 'This is a character who only knows one thing – how to use her body to get what she wants.'

GF: *That explains the sequence outside the rock venue when she gets in for free by preening in front of the doorman.*

HH: Yes. And later on, at Grand Central Station, when she's put Edward's life at risk and is desperately trying to get him away from there. She starts seducing him, first politely, and then getting more and more raunchy. But it backfires completely and she's left feeling ridiculous.

I don't think I would have found myself making a story that dealt with these particular issues if I didn't believe that a lot of people consider that I write strong female roles. I know that, and I appreciate a lot of the insight people give me on that, but I also know that I am very confused by a lot of the writing about my films. Women represented as sex objects? Yes, I am participating in it and questioning my participation in it at the same time. Maybe that's not fair, but fairness isn't the point.

GF: *Your films are scarcely indulgent on this level. In terms of sex and violence, they remain highly restrained.*

HH: Titillation is too easy. It immediately unplugs everything that's interesting.

GF: *In your diary, on May 8, 1993, you wrote about visiting a topless bar and speaking to Maria, a dancer there who had seen two of your films and said that they 'made her feel my respect for women, but not my lust. I added that perhaps I was just embarrassed by my lust and needed to dignify it by turning it into love stories.'*

HH: I went to topless bars a number of times while writing *Amateur*, and one of the things I noticed the most was that it was not about sexual arousal at all. To me, it seemed a situation where you have the ability to exercise your options in a way that you don't in the outside world. That's the attraction for a man. Men can go there and they can choose to spend money on a girl dancing topless or they can choose not to do it. If it was exciting, it was exciting about money and opportunity, not about sex. I could be there because I could afford to be there.

GF: *In the movie, Sofia and Thomas have clearly been deadened by making pornographic films. They've been anaesthetized, not as consumers, but as suppliers.*

HH: All this stuff is very much like a drug. I compare it to drugs and drinking a lot. As a consumer, you can never get enough, and it just gets less and less interesting. I have no moral compunction about pornography per se. Ultimately, the best and worst I can say about it is that it's beside the point. There was an exchange between Thomas and Isabelle in the script that I shot, but finally cut out. Isabelle had asked Thomas the same question about the magazines that he later asks the boy in the park, 'Do you find these women attractive?' Thomas replied to her that they embarrassed him; that they seemed to be trying to prove something that they didn't believe themselves. It was

horrible; insincere. I was being affected by the knowledge of my
own relative celebrity. It sounded like something I was
supposed to say.

GF: *In your final diary note you made during the making of this
film, you stated, on January 16, 1994: 'Ultimately, I want to make
images that take nothing for granted, images that by virtue of their
singularity provide the most avenues of interpretation, images that
are clear, but not obvious.' Did you feel you succeeded?*

HH: I don't know. Maybe. I'm moved by some of the most
normal shots. The angle on Isabelle with the coffee cup, for
example. She's sitting on the edge of the bed when Martin
wakes up in her apartment and it's a very simple single. It has
everything to do with Isabelle Huppert. What she allows to be
seen. What she retains. The time she takes. That's something I
really learned from editing Isabelle – the time that she takes.
She knows that she can sustain it. There is a state of the soul
that she loans to her character. It's almost like a physical
knowledge. I talked a lot about gesture – the kind of gesture
that is calculated – before Isabelle and I worked together, but
she doesn't like to talk about it much and I'm glad I was ready –
I had time to prepare myself, unknowingly – to work with
someone who really understands what I mean.

GF: *She fits seamlessly into the rarefied world of your movies.*
Yes. Her screen presence is amazing, whether you know who
she is or not. I'm quite fond of that initial image of Isabelle
writing on her computer in the coffee shop.

GF: *A moment later, Thomas enters the room and you hold an
angle down on him as he sits and slings his change on the counter.
Although we've seen him in the opening shot, it's that angle and
the abruptness of his action that said to me, 'This is Martin
Donovan and he's telling us that we're watching a Hal Hartley
film.'*

HH: Whenever Martin comes by the editing room, we all start
shouting, 'Look out! He's in the house! Martin Donovan is in
the house!' And that shot's definitely a 'Look-out-Martin-
Donovan's-in-the-house!' shot. There was a consciousness of
that in making the movie.

GF: *It's exactly the kind of thing that inspired a friend of mine to say
that watching your movies is like being part of a club.*

HH: Not too exclusive, I hope.

10 'I'm quite fond of that initial image of Isabelle writing on her computer in the coffee shop.'

11 'Look out, Martin Donovan's in the house!'

Cast

Isabelle	Isabelle Huppert
Thomas	Martin Donovan
Sofia	Elina Lowensohn
Edward	Damian Young
Jan	Chuck Montgomery
Kurt	David Simonds
Officer Melville	Pamela Stewart
Irate Woman	Erica Gimpel
Waitress	Jan Leslie Harding
Frank, the Cook	Terry Alexander
Usher	Holt McCallany
Warren	Hugh Palmer
Doorman at Club	Michael Imperioli
Detective	Angel Caban
Bartender	Emmanuel Xuereb
Taxi Driver	Lennie Loftin
George, The Pornographer	David Greenspan
Kid Reading the Odyssey	Adria Tennor
Girl Squatter	Parker Posey
Boy Squatter	Dwight Ewell
Video Store Clerk	Currie Graham
Pizza Guy	Jamie Harrold
Young Irate Mother	Patricia Scanlon
Policeman #1	James McCauley
Policeman #2	Benny Nieves
Guard	David Troup
Young Detective	Tim Blake Nelson
Sister at Door	Marissa Copeland
Mother Superior	Dael Orlandersmith
Sharp Shooter in Bush	Michael Gaston
Cop who shoots Thomas	Paul Schulze

Cinematographer	Michael Spiller
Production Designer	Steven Rosenzweig
Editor	Steven Hamilton
Music	Ned Rifle & Jeffrey Taylor
Executive Producers	Jerome Brownstein
	Scott Meek
	Yves Marmion
	Lindsay Law
Produced by	Hal Hartley & Ted Hope
Written & Directed by	Hal Hartley

A Zenita/True Fiction Pictures Production

EXT. COBBLESTONE STREET. MORNING.

It's raining.
A 33-year-old man, THOMAS, *is lying in the middle of an empty*
and old street, dead.
A young woman, SOFIA, *appears around the corner, breathless and*
frightened. She approaches THOMAS *carefully.*
There's a small pool of blood beneath his head and when SOFIA
nudges him with her foot she can sense the limpness of death and
backs away. She looks around to see if anyone is a witness to this,
but seeing no one, glances back at THOMAS *and covers her mouth.*
Trembling, she turns and runs away up the street . . .

TITLES.

Back in the street, the wind sweeps over THOMAS's *sprawled body*
as rain water streams past him through the gutter.
But then his eyes open.
He turns his head slowly and looks to either side. This hurts and he
raises a hand to the back of his head. But this hurts too and he
doubles up and holds his rib cage. Finally, he sits on the curb and
looks up and down the street . . .

I

ISABELLE: (*Off*) 'And this man will die . . . He will.
    Eventually.'

INT. COFFEE SHOP. LATER THAT DAY.

ISABELLE *is a pale, undernourished 33-year-old woman sitting at*
the counter and writing on a lap-top computer. She is pretty, but
plain and dressed poorly.
She types feverishly away, reciting as she goes . . .
ISABELLE: (*Continues*) ' "He will die," she repeated, "and there
    is nothing any of us can do about it." Vera put the last of
    the bullets into the chamber of the gun and stood in the
    window to keep an eye on the street below.' (*Pauses to light*
    a cigarette.) 'Frank's calloused hand worked its way up
    under her tight fitting skirt and caressed her perfect ass. He
    pulled her back against himself and she felt his cock against
    her, like a piece of two-by-four in his trousers.'
    (*A* WOMAN *at a nearby table jumps up.*)
WOMAN: Listen, lady, you better settle down! You're
    embarrassing my friend!
ISABELLE: (*To* WAITRESS) Excuse me, can I have another coffee
    please?
WAITRESS: (*Screams*) You can't sit here all day, you know!
ISABELLE: I pay for my coffee.
WAITRESS: You buy one or two cups of coffee and you sit there
    all day! Day after day! You take up space!
ISABELLE: I bought one of those muffins this morning.
WAITRESS: You did not.
ISABELLE: I did.
WAITRESS: Which kind?
ISABELLE: (*Points*) That kind.
FRANK: (*The cook*) Ah, leave her alone! She's harmless!
WAITRESS: (*Moves off*) This is not a hotel!
ISABELLE: (*Adds*) It had mold on it.
    (*But then she sees . . .*
    THOMAS *limp into the Coffee Shop.*
    ISABELLE *is immediately captivated. She looks on as . . .*)
WAITRESS: Can I help you?
    (THOMAS *can't yet form the words to answer and he looks*
    around, confused.)

2

WAITRESS: Come on, pal, what'll it be!
(*He finds some change in his trouser pocket and dumps it all on the counter.*
The WAITRESS *lifts one of the coins and frowns at him.*)
WAITRESS: This is no good. What kinda money is this? (*Turns to the cook.*) What kind of money is this, Frank?
FRANK: (*Looks*) Dutch.
(*She looks at* THOMAS.)
WAITRESS: Are you Dutch?
THOMAS: I don't know.
FRANK: He sounds like an American.
WAITRESS: Where'd you get this Dutch money?
THOMAS: It was in my pocket.
WAITRESS: Look, take your Dutch money and get outta here!
ISABELLE: (*Approaches*) He's hurt.
WAITRESS: What?
ISABELLE: He's bleeding. Bring some water.
ISABELLE: (*To* THOMAS) Does it hurt?
THOMAS: Yes.
WAITRESS: Do you know your name?
THOMAS: No.
ISABELLE: (*Working*) Keep still.
(*He keeps still.*)

3

WAITRESS: (*Amazed*) Frank, he doesn't know his name.
  (FRANK *shrugs.*
  ISABELLE *carefully daubs at the back of* THOMAS's *head.
  Then . . .*)
ISABELLE: Are you hungry?
THOMAS: Yes.
  (ISABELLE *steps away and gets her purse. She removes a five
  dollar bill and carefully, ceremoniously, offers it to the*
  WAITRESS.)
ISABELLE: A sandwich, please.
  (*The* WAITRESS *takes the money, surprised.*)
WAITRESS: Hey, look, Frank, she's got money!
  (ISABELLE *and* THOMAS *both turn around to face each other
  for a long moment.*)

INT. COFFEE SHOP. A LITTLE LATER.

ISABELLE *and* THOMAS *are sitting at the counter.*
ISABELLE: Did you have enough to eat?
THOMAS: Yes. Thank you. You want some?
ISABELLE: No.
THOMAS: You sure?
ISABELLE: Yes.
  (ISABELLE *gets up and walks around to face him.*)
ISABELLE: D'you smoke?
THOMAS: I don't know.
  (*She taps a cigarette out for herself . . .*)
ISABELLE: I just started smoking. It helps me forget I'm
  hungry.
THOMAS: Well, then eat some of this.
ISABELLE: No, I couldn't.
THOMAS: Why not?
ISABELLE: I'm not hungry.
THOMAS: You're only forgetting you're hungry because of the
  cigarettes.
ISABELLE: Yes, I know. But I had a muffin too.
THOMAS: When?
ISABELLE: Before.
  (*He doesn't believe her, but lets it go.* ISABELLE *sits down next
  to him.*)

4

THOMAS: I was reading your story.

ISABELLE: Did you like it?

THOMAS: It's sad.

ISABELLE: Yes. Everything I write comes out sad. Why do you
think that is?

THOMAS: (*Firmly*) I don't know. Look, eat this.
(*And he makes her take the sandwich. He takes the cigarette.
After a little hesitation,* ISABELLE *takes a bite. Satisfied,*
THOMAS *grabs a pack of matches off the counter.*)

ISABELLE: You have no identification?

THOMAS: No. I woke up in the street. I don't know how I got
there.
(THOMAS *lights up.*)

ISABELLE: Perhaps you were robbed.

THOMAS: Could be.

ISABELLE: Maybe you tried to commit suicide?

THOMAS: (*Smokes*) You think so?

ISABELLE: (*Excited, notices*) You know how.

THOMAS: Excuse me?

ISABELLE: You know how to smoke. It took me a few weeks to
learn how to inhale.
(THOMAS *notices.*)

THOMAS: Did I inhale?

ISABELLE: (*Nods*) Yes.
(*He considers the cigarette in his hand, then remembers the
sandwich.*)

THOMAS: Eat that.
(*She continues eating.* THOMAS *studies the pack of
matches.*)
(*Reads.*) 'Hot Phone Sex.'

ISABELLE: You can keep them if you want.
(*Uncertain, but gracious, he puts them in his pocket and notices
the magazines.*)

THOMAS: And what are these?

ISABELLE: Pornographic magazines.

THOMAS: Can I look at one?

ISABELLE: Sure. I met this man, George, who said he'd pay me
to write some of these short stories they publish.
(THOMAS *finds one of these stories. He reads . . .*)

THOMAS: 'He reached out a hand and grabbed her chin, forcing

5

his fingers brutally into her cheeks as he lifted her face
towards his.'

(ISABELLE *watches him as he reads*.)

THOMAS: ' "I never use the same woman twice," he said, "any
more than I'd smoke the same cigarette twice. You're used
up. I've gotten all I need or want out of you." ' (*To*
ISABELLE.) That ever happen to you?

ISABELLE: (*Feels ill suddenly*) No.

EXT. COFFEE SHOP. MOMENTS LATER.

ISABELLE *is throwing up*.

THOMAS *stands aside*.

The WAITRESS *is watching from a few yards off*.

WAITRESS: She never eats anything! That's what the problem is!

THOMAS: (*Tries to get rid of her*) Thank you!

WAITRESS: You gotta have some food in your gut to build up
resistance to the heat and humidity!

THOMAS: Right.

(ISABELLE *is through being sick and begins to walk*.
The WAITRESS *moves off*.
ISABELLE *rests with her back against a wall, slowly sinking
down*. THOMAS *crouches down beside her*.)

ISABELLE: (*To* THOMAS) I'm sorry.

THOMAS: What for?

ISABELLE: (*Finally*) I should go back to the convent.

THOMAS: (*Surprised*) You're a nun?

ISABELLE: No. (*Coughs, pauses, looks away.*) Not anymore.
(*He watches her rest a moment, then looks up and down the street.*)

INT. ISABELLE'S PLACE. AN HOUR LATER.

It's a wretched little east village hovel.

ISABELLE *comes in, sick and cold, and immediately falls upon the bed.* THOMAS *closes the door.*

ISABELLE *gets up, not letting herself rest.*

ISABELLE: I have some antiseptic for your cuts. (*She gets off the bed and goes into the bathroom.*) Can you remember anything at all about who you are?
(*He sighs and thinks, trying to piece his feelings together.*
ISABELLE *comes out of the bathroom and watches him.*)

THOMAS: I feel things. But I don't know what they mean. No. I don't remember. I'm confused, mostly.

ISABELLE: Are you frightened?

THOMAS: Frightened?

ISABELLE: Yes. Scared.

THOMAS: Of what?
(*At a loss, she shrugs.*)

ISABELLE: I don't know. (*She goes to the door and sets the chain lock, then looks back at* THOMAS *and pauses.*) So you don't remember anything? No feelings, no caresses, no kisses, no . . .

THOMAS: No.
(ISABELLE *pauses uneasily, then she looks at her watch.*)

ISABELLE: I have a date.

THOMAS: I should go. Thank you.

ISABELLE: No. Don't leave. We can go to the police in the morning. You can stay here tonight.

THOMAS: Alright. I'll sleep on the floor.

ISABELLE: No.

THOMAS: I don't mind.

ISABELLE: I have no blankets for you if you sleep on the floor.

7

THOMAS: I'll use my jacket.

ISABELLE: But you can sleep in the bed with me.

    (*He considers the bed, then . . .*)

THOMAS: There's no room in the bed for the two of us.

    (ISABELLE *estimates the bed as well.*)

ISABELLE: There is. If we lie very close together.

    (THOMAS *turns his head to* ISABELLE *as she hesitantly meets his stare.*)

THOMAS: Who do you have a date with?

ISABELLE: I don't know. His name is Warren. I've only spoken to him on the hot phone-sex party line.

INT. MOVIE THEATER. EVENING.

The entrance doors open to reveal ISABELLE *and* WARREN, *an infinitely normal-looking guy. As they look for a seat,* ISABELLE *sees . . .*

SOFIA *asleep in a seat straight across from her.*

She sees that . . .

SOFIA's *purse has dropped to the floor beneath her seat.*

Careful not to wake SOFIA, ISABELLE *steps over and reaches down to retrieve the purse. She places it securely within the curve of* SOFIA's *arm.*

An USHER *approaches and shines a flashlight at the girl.*

USHER: Hey. Hey, come on. Get up.

    (SOFIA *wakes with a start and looks up at him, terrified.*)

USHER: This is not a hotel. You've been in here all day. Get up and get outta here!

    (SOFIA *rises upward in her seat and pulls herself together.*

    ISABELLE *calls to the* USHER.)

ISABELLE: But there are so many seats here no one is sitting in.

USHER: Listen, lady, mind your own business!

    (SOFIA *looks from the* USHER *to* ISABELLE, *pauses, then walks out, followed by the* USHER.

    ISABELLE *watches them go. Then, startled, she looks down at . . .*

    WARREN's *hand on her knee. He slides it up her leg.*)

ISABELLE: What are you doing?

WARREN: I'm molesting you.

    (*Breathless, she looks up at him.*)

8

ISABELLE: Am I supposed to like it?
WARREN: You could beg me to stop.
ISABELLE: And would you?
WARREN: No.
ISABELLE: I have to go.
   (*And she gets up and runs out.*)

EXT. MOVIE THEATER. MOMENTS LATER.

SOFIA *stands at a phone booth, listening to the dial tone. She looks over as . . .*
ISABELLE *comes out of the theater, looks at her, and then wanders away, troubled.*
There is no answer, and SOFIA *slams the receiver down.*

EXT. CBGB'S. NIGHT.

JAMES *is a wiry twenty-five-year-old aspiring rock guitarist working the door. A female rock fan pays him to enter the dark cavern of pulsating noise.*
JAMES: Thank you. (*He stamps the back of her hand with a little rubber stamp.*) Enjoy.
   (*Sofia comes up and walks back and forth in front of the entrance.*
   JAMES *watches her, checking her out.*
   She's aware of this. She comes closer.)
SOFIA: Who's playing?
JAMES: Some band from Seattle.
SOFIA: Are they good?
JAMES: I guess. I can't hear too well.
SOFIA: You must get bored out here.
JAMES: I only have to work the door till ten.
   (*Some students come up and start reaching for their wallets.*)
JAMES: Have your ID please. Thanks. (*Off-screen.*) Thank you. Enjoy the show.
   (SOFIA *waits, smoking. The* STUDENTS *file in and, when the door closes,* JAMES *and* SOFIA *are left alone again in an awkward silence.*)
JAMES: You wanna see the show?
SOFIA: I can't afford ten dollars.

9

JAMES: Here. Go on in anyway.
(*He takes his little stamp pad and brands the back of her hand.*)
SOFIA: Thank you.
JAMES: It's OK. The management wants a lot of good-looking women in the place. It's good for business.
(*She looks at her little stamp, and then up at* JAMES.)
SOFIA: I know.
(*She enters.*)

INT. ISABELLE'S BATHROOM/APT. LATER.

THOMAS *is in the bathtub, reading a pornographic magazine. He looks at a picture, then shakes his head, impressed, but bothered, and turns the page. He turns around as . . .*
ISABELLE *enters the apartment, frustrated, and stands in the bathroom door.*
THOMAS: How was your date?
ISABELLE: I think there's something wrong with me.
(THOMAS *closes the magazine and throws it down on the floor.*)
THOMAS: (*Looks up*) How long has it been since you left the convent, Isabelle?
ISABELLE: Ten months.
THOMAS: How long were you a nun?
ISABELLE: Fifteen years.
THOMAS: That's a long time.
(*She steps into the bathroom and takes out her cigarettes.*)
ISABELLE: When I make mistakes they tend to be big ones.
THOMAS: Were you always religious?
ISABELLE: No.
(*She lights a cigarette.*)
ISABELLE: When I was a girl I wasted a lot of time writing bad poetry about being lonely and too fat.
THOMAS: You were fat, huh?
ISABELLE: Not so fat. But I was ugly. (*Pauses for a moment, then . . .*) Well, anyway, it was around that time that the Virgin Mary began appearing to me.
(THOMAS *looks up.*)
THOMAS: (*Uncertain*) Pardon me?
ISABELLE: It's true. She appeared to me three times in one year.

II

THOMAS: (*Washing his chest*) And what did she say?

ISABELLE: She said I should not become a nun.

THOMAS: Why?

ISABELLE: Because I'm a nymphomaniac.

THOMAS: What?

ISABELLE: It's true.

THOMAS: You don't look like one.

ISABELLE: Like a nymphomaniac?

THOMAS: Yeah.

ISABELLE: How would you know?
  (*She's got a point.* THOMAS *considers it and looks away.*
  ISABELLE *sits.*)

ISABELLE: But I lied. I told the priest God wanted me to join
  the order and become a nun.

THOMAS: After all that?

ISABELLE: Well, I was scared.

THOMAS: Of what?

ISABELLE: I was scared of what I knew God had planned for
  me.

THOMAS: God had something planned for you, huh?

ISABELLE: Yes.

THOMAS: What?

ISABELLE: I don't know yet. The Virgin didn't tell me that. But
  she did say it's going to be difficult. It's going to hurt. And
  I need to be out here in the world to do it. Not in a
  convent.
  (*She takes off her jacket.*)
  I was seventeen. I was scared. So I lied. I lied for fifteen
  years. I lied until I couldn't bear it any longer.

THOMAS: (*impressed*) Shit.
  (ISABELLE *pauses thoughtfully for a moment, then* . . .)

ISABELLE: Will you make love to me?

THOMAS: When?

ISABELLE: When you finish your bath.

THOMAS: Why me?

ISABELLE: Why not you?

THOMAS: Well, you don't know me. You don't even know my
  name.

ISABELLE: You don't know your name either.
  (*He thinks about this.*)

THOMAS: Have you ever *had* sex?

ISABELLE: No.

THOMAS: How can you be a nymphomaniac and never had sex?

ISABELLE: (*Smokes, then . . .*) I'm choosy.

(THOMAS *frowns, rubbing his stubbled jaw.*)

THOMAS: I need to shave.

(*She reaches over to the sink and gets him a lady-shick disposable razor.*)

ISABELLE: Is this OK? I use it on my legs.

(THOMAS *takes it and lathers up.*

She watches him. After a while, he glances over at her . . .)

THOMAS: I don't think you're a nymphomaniac.

ISABELLE: You don't?

THOMAS: No.

ISABELLE: So, you'll make love to me?

(*He cuts himself shaving and winces in pain.*)

ISABELLE: I did the same thing yesterday. Here.

(*And she shows him a small cut on her leg. He looks at it, then up at her.*)

THOMAS: I think I'm in too much pain to make love tonight.

ISABELLE: I can wait. I've waited all my life.

INT. JAMES'S APT. NEXT MORNING.

JAMES *is still asleep on a mattress on the floor of his tiny one-room apartment.*

SOFIA *sits at the edge of the mattress, lacing up her boots. She gets up and grabs the phone. Stepping into the bathroom, she closes the door and dials.*

Finally . . .

SOFIA: (*Whispers*) Edward? . . . It's Sofia . . . Yes. I'm here in New York . . . I can't talk now. Can I see you? . . . No.
(*Pauses, closes her eyes, and takes a big breath, then . . .*)
Thomas is dead . . . Yes.

INT. ISABELLE'S APT. MORNING.

THOMAS *is still sleeping.*

ISABELLE *is sitting up at the edge of the bed looking down upon*

13

him, holding a cup of coffee. After watching him a few moments,
she reaches out and caresses his shoulder.
He jumps up, startled, and ISABELLE *jumps back in alarm.*
THOMAS: ARRGGHHH!!!
> (*But he realizes where he is, freezes, then relaxes. He looks at*
> ISABELLE, *embarrassed.*
> *She watches him without moving.*
> *Finally . . .*)
THOMAS: Sorry.
> (*He sits back against the wall.*)
ISABELLE: You talk in your sleep.
THOMAS: I do?
ISABELLE: Yes.
THOMAS: What did I say?
ISABELLE: Have some coffee.
THOMAS: What did I say?
ISABELLE: (*Hesitates*) You were shouting at someone named
Sofia.
> (THOMAS *frowns, thinking carefully. Finally . . .*)
THOMAS: Sofia?
ISABELLE: (*Worried*) Do you remember her?
THOMAS: (*Thinks, then*) No.
ISABELLE: (*Relieved*) How do you feel?
THOMAS: A little better.
ISABELLE: Good.
THOMAS: We should go to the police.
ISABELLE: No. Why?
THOMAS: Someone's probably looking for me.
ISABELLE: (*Pauses, then*) This Sofia person maybe?
THOMAS: Yeah. Maybe.
> (ISABELLE *thinks, takes a sip of coffee, then . . .*)
ISABELLE: You were very mean to her. I doubt she'd miss
you.
THOMAS: Oh, yeah?
ISABELLE: Yes. Very mean.
THOMAS: How?
> (ISABELLE *takes another sip of coffee.*)
ISABELLE: (*Reluctant*) You were threatening to hurt her.
THOMAS: What did I say? (*No response, then . . .*) Isabelle, what
did I say in my sleep?

ISABELLE: (*Finally*) You said you were going to slice up her face
with a razor blade.
(THOMAS *is stunned. He looks around, clearly troubled.*)

INT. CAFE. LATER THAT MORNING.

SOFIA *is sitting at a table, talking to* EDWARD (*off-screen*).

SOFIA: I hate him. He took advantage of me. He got me hooked on
drugs when I was twelve. He put me in pornographic films.
I'm sick of it. I want to change my life. He won't let me. I'm
unhappy. I pushed him out a window. I killed him.
(EDWARD *is stunned. He's a harried-looking man of about
forty who drinks too much. He talks to* SOFIA *over his
shoulder.*)

EDWARD: When was this?

SOFIA: Yesterday morning.

EDWARD: Here in New York?

SOFIA: Yes.

EDWARD: How did he know you were in New York?

SOFIA: I don't know. He knew everything.

EDWARD: What did he want?

SOFIA: He was angry because I left him. He said if I didn't
come back he was going to 'disfigure' me.
(EDWARD *looks up in mild horror.*)
He showed me some pictures. (*She shrugs.*) Stuff they do to
girls.
(EDWARD *considers all this. He watches her and sighs, then
looks away, thinking.*)

EDWARD: What are you gonna do?

SOFIA: I don't know. (*She looks around for a moment, then . . .*)
Tell me about Jacques.

EDWARD: Jacques?

SOFIA: Yes.

EDWARD: How do you know about Jacques?

SOFIA: Thomas mentioned him.

EDWARD: Oh, yeah, what did he say?

SOFIA: Not much. But I know Thomas got money from him to
make the movies.
(EDWARD *is reluctant. He sits back and looks into the street.*)

EDWARD: He's a business man.

15

SOFIA: What did you do for him?

EDWARD: (*Defensive*) Look, I didn't do anything for him! I'm an accountant! I took care of Thomas's money!

SOFIA: Is what Jacques does illegal?

EDWARD: Look, the less you know about Jacques the better. Forget anything Thomas said about Jacques.

SOFIA: I think Thomas was in trouble with Jacques.

EDWARD: Yeah, Thomas was in trouble with everyone.

SOFIA: Why?

EDWARD: Because he's the devil.

SOFIA: No, I mean why was he in trouble with Jacques?

(EDWARD *hesitates. Finally . . .*)

EDWARD: Thomas tried to blackmail him.

SOFIA: With what?

EDWARD: Accounting documents. Records of banking transactions, stuff like that.

SOFIA: So Jacques did something illegal?

EDWARD: He's an arms dealer.

SOFIA: And that's not allowed?

EDWARD: It depends. Not always. In this case, definitely not.

SOFIA: What do the documents look like?

EDWARD: Why, do you know where they are?

SOFIA: I don't know.

EDWARD: They're floppy disks.

SOFIA: Floppy disks.

EDWARD: Yeah, you know, like . . . (*He takes some discs out of his bag.*) like these.

(*She takes them and looks them over.*)

SOFIA: This is what you call a floppy disk?

EDWARD: Yeah.

SOFIA: But it's square.

EDWARD: Yeah, yeah I know, but they call them floppy disks.

SOFIA: It's not floppy either. It's stiff.

EDWARD: (*Annoyed*) Look, Sofia, did you ever see Thomas with anything that looks like these?

SOFIA: (*Gives it back*) No.

(*His cellular phone rings and he whips it open . . .*)

EDWARD: Hello. Yeah. What? No way. Right. (*He gets up and excuses himself.*) I'll be right back.

(*And he goes out of the café.*

16

SOFIA *waits a few moments, then she carefully reaches over and opens his brief case.*
She pokes around a little, then finds what she's looking for . . .
His phone book.
She flips through it and finds . . .
Jacques's number.
She copies it down onto a napkin and replaces the phone book.
EDWARD *returns. As he sits, he takes out his pen and note pad.*)
EDWARD: Sorry about that.

(SOFIA *tries to make light conversation.*)
SOFIA: So what do you do now that you're back in the States?
EDWARD: (*Taking out his wallet*) I prepare people's taxes.
SOFIA: (*Brightly*) Oh, that sounds so interesting.

(*He glances at her in disbelief as he begins to write in his note pad.*)
EDWARD: Look, this is the address of a house one of my clients owns upstate in a town called Portchester. No one's there. You go by train this afternoon, you take a taxi from the station, pick up some groceries to last a couple of days. (*He gives her some money.*) Oh, here's fifty bucks. Now you get there and stay put till we see what happens.
SOFIA: How will I get in?
EDWARD: I'll get the key from my office and I'll meet you at the station.

(*She leans over and gives him a kiss.*)
SOFIA: Thank you, Edward. I know you must not think that much of me.
EDWARD: No. You're wrong. Anyone who would kill Thomas is a friend of mine. He's ruined our lives.
SOFIA: No. He hasn't. He damaged them. But I'm going to change all that. I'm going to change my life. And I'll help you too. I'm going to take charge of things. (*Takes a triumphant fix off her cigarette, then . . .*) I'm going to be a mover and a shaker. You wait and see.

INT. POLICE STATION. EARLY AFTERNOON.

THOMAS *has his picture taken.*
OFFICER MELVILLE, *a strangely sensitive and violently emotional woman, tries to reassure him . . .*

OFFICER MELVILLE: That's all we can do for the time being. No one has reported a person fitting your description as missing. But if they do, at least now we have your picture. (*She looks at him and sighs sadly.*) Do you have a place to stay?

(THOMAS *looks at* ISABELLE. *She nods.*)

THOMAS: (*To* MELVILLE) Yes. Thank you.

OFFICER MELVILLE: (*Relieved*) Oh, good. I hate to have to bring people in your position across the street to the Hospital. (*Looks away, crushed.*) It's so cold and unfeeling over there. So hopeless and, frankly, under-staffed.

(THOMAS *and* ISABELLE *watch, quietly, and politely, amazed. The* DETECTIVE *who has been working behind her leans forward and addresses her.*)

DETECTIVE: Let's go, Melville! Don't start crying!

OFFICER MELVILLE: OK! OK!

DETECTIVE: You're an officer of the law!

(*She looks up, indignant, but then controls herself and looks back at* THOMAS.)

OFFICER MELVILLE: Take care. Good luck.

THOMAS: Thank you.

(*She runs out just after he leaves, unable to keep herself from crying.*)

INT. CAFE. SAME TIME.

SOFIA *sashays up to the bar and gets the attention of the* BARTENDER.

SOFIA: Hello, may I use your phone?

BARTENDER: There's a pay phone by the rest room.

SOFIA: Yes, I know. But I have no change.

BARTENDER: Is it a local call?

SOFIA: Not really, but I'll be brief.

(*She takes the phone, steps away dials, waits, then . . .*)

SOFIA: Hello, I'd like to call the Netherlands.

OPERATOR: What is the number, please?

SOFIA: 31 20 626 1155

(*She waves to the bartender as she waits and is finally connected.*)

RECEPTIONIST: (*Dutch*) 'Good afternoon. Bad organization.'

SOFIA: Hello. May I speak to Mister Jacques please?
RECEPTIONIST: (*English*) Who may I say is calling?
SOFIA: You can tell him Sofia Ludens is calling.
> (*She waits.*
> *Eventually,* JACQUES *picks up.*)
JACQUES: Yes?
SOFIA: Is this Mister Jacques?
JACQUES: Who is this?
SOFIA: This is Sofia Ludens. I'm Thomas's wife.
JACQUES: I know who you are.
SOFIA: So, is this Mister Jacques?
JACQUES: That depends.
SOFIA: On what?
JACQUES: Is Thomas with you?
SOFIA: No.
JACQUES: Where are you calling from?
SOFIA: I can't tell you that.
JACQUES: Why are you calling, Sofia?
SOFIA: I need to tell Mister Jacques something important.
JACQUES: Can you tell me?
SOFIA: Are you Mister Jacques?
JACQUES: Yes.
SOFIA: How do I know that?
JACQUES: You have no choice.
> (*She looks away, frustrated, and considers this. Then* . . .)
SOFIA: Look, I have something that belongs to Mister
   Jacques.
JACQUES: Like what?
> (*She swallows and has to struggle for breath before she finally*
> *manages to mumble* . . .)
SOFIA: Floppy disks.
> (*Silence.*
> *She waits. She looks at the receiver.*
> *Still no response. Finally* . . .)
JACQUES: What do you want, Sofia?
SOFIA: Money.
JACQUES: How much money?
> (*She didn't expect all this. She thinks quickly, desperately,*
> *then* . . .)
SOFIA: (*Guessing*) A million dollars.

JACQUES: OK.
> (*Her jaw drops. She waits, then . . .*)
Can you come here to our offices?
SOFIA: (*Breathless*) No. No. I'm not in Amsterdam.
JACQUES: It doesn't matter. We have contacts all over the world.
SOFIA: Somewhere public.
JACQUES: Do you have the floppy disks with you?
SOFIA: No, but I can tell you where they are.
JACQUES: Fine. But where do we find you?
> (*She hesitates, trying to think, then . . .*)
SOFIA: New York City.
JACQUES: Where in New York City?
> (*She looks out the window, exhausted. But she pulls herself together, thinks, and decides.*)
SOFIA: At Grand Central Station.

EXT. STREET. MOMENTS LATER.

THOMAS *is troubled.* ISABELLE *is too. They walk a while, but then she stops. He walks on a few paces before noticing and turning back. Finally, she looks out at the passing traffic.*
ISABELLE: What will you do when you find out who you are?
THOMAS: I can't say.
> (*She looks up at him. After a moment . . .*)
ISABELLE: You have a little scar here, just above the eye.
THOMAS: I do?
ISABELLE: I like it.
THOMAS: Thanks.
ISABELLE: You have to make love to me before you remember your name.
THOMAS: Well, I feel a little better today. Why don't we go back to your place and make love right now?
> (*She smiles, but then . . .*)
ISABELLE: I have to go read my short story to George the pornographer.
THOMAS: What about me?
ISABELLE: Would you like to look at one of my magazines?
> (*She gives him one. He flips through it, bored.*)
ISABELLE: Meet me outside my building at five.

INT. GRAND CENTRAL STATION. 2PM.

SOFIA *comes skipping across the main concourse of the station,
tossing her head to the music on her walkman. Moments later, she
enters the cafe which overlooks the station and finds* EDWARD.

SOFIA: Hello!

EDWARD: You're in a good mood.

SOFIA: (*Gives him flowers*) Yes. I am in a good mood. These are
  for you.
  (SOFIA *moves to the café entrance, and looks over at . . .*
  *A man in a business suit standing in the station entrance. He is
  wearing dark glasses and carrying a briefcase.*
  *She watches him closely, expecting he may be someone sent by
  Mister Jacques.*
  *The man has been looking out into the street, but now turns to
  face the station, looking in* SOFIA's *general direction.*
  *The man may be looking at her, but he doesn't register
  anything.*
  SOFIA *waits until . . .*
  *The man is met by a woman. He takes off his glasses and they
  kiss before walking off out of the station.*
  Relieved and disappointed, SOFIA *sighs and returns to*
  EDWARD.

21

She gets back up on the bar stool as EDWARD *removes the headphones and leans forward.*)

EDWARD: By the way, Sofia, if anyone asks about those floppy disks, or mentions Mister Jacques, you just make like you never heard about any of it. OK?

SOFIA: Sure.

EDWARD: I mean, not even to your closest friend.

SOFIA: (*Smiles*) You're my closest friend.

EDWARD: (*Genuine*) Thank you.

SOFIA: Besides, I'm good at keeping secrets.

EDWARD: That's good.

SOFIA: I learned all sorts of criminal-type behaviour from Thomas.

EDWARD: Oh yeah, like what?

(*She almost starts to recite a list, but then gives up.*)

SOFIA: I'd rather not talk about it. It was pretty disgusting.

(EDWARD *nods, understanding. He drinks.*)

EDWARD: How did you meet Thomas, anyway?

SOFIA: Through my sister. She used to travel around with these rock'n'roll bands. I left home and joined her.

EDWARD: You were a groupie.

SOFIA: Yes. But then my sister died of an overdose and the band threw me off the bus in the middle of nowhere. That's when I met Thomas and he got me into the movie thing.

EDWARD: And you were twelve years old then?

SOFIA: Almost thirteen.

(EDWARD *shakes his head, drinks, then* . . .)

EDWARD: We were good pornographers there for a while. At least, I thought so. Had offices in London, Amsterdam and Miami. We made a product of a certain quality, we paid our bills on time. We made profits. We got rich, actually.

SOFIA: What made you quit?

EDWARD: I had no choice. I was trying to save my life.

SOFIA: I don't understand.

EDWARD: It's true. Jacques will kill anyone who even knows about those floppy disks.

(SOFIA *freezes.*)

SOFIA: Excuse me?

EDWARD: I tried to tell him this. I tried to tell him he was

risking my life as well as his own. Risking your life.
Risking the lives of everybody who worked with us. But he
didn't care. He didn't care about anybody.

SOFIA: But they didn't kill you?

EDWARD: They didn't kill me because they don't know where I
am.

(*Her mind is racing. She stands, going pale.*)

SOFIA: We should go now.

EDWARD: I'll walk you to the train.

SOFIA: No. I'm OK. Go home.

EDWARD: I don't wanna go home. I'm enjoying myself.

SOFIA: You've got to go home, Edward. You should be hiding.

EDWARD: Ah, they still think I'm in Europe.

(SOFIA *is feverishly scanning the station entrance. She comes
back and sits again, leaning in close.*)

SOFIA: Come with me, then.

EDWARD: What?

SOFIA: Come with me to the country.

EDWARD: Now?

SOFIA: Yes. Now. Come on, we've got to hurry!

(*Now there are two particular men,* JAN *and* KURT, *more alert
and threatening than the others, standing in the station entrance
and looking around.*)

SOFIA: Aren't we having a good time?

EDWARD: Yeah, we're having a great time.

SOFIA: I feel so close to you all of a sudden. Please come with
me.

(EDWARD *is surprised and embarrassed, but . . .*)

EDWARD: Sure.

SOFIA: Good! Let's go!

(*She turns back.*)

EDWARD: But there really are one or two things I gotta take care
of at the office before I go.

(*On the steps near the concourse,* KURT *grabs a young woman
who looks fairly like* SOFIA. *He turns her around violently, sees
it's not her, and continues on.
Meanwhile, in the café . . .*)

EDWARD: (*To* SOFIA) I'll call you at the house as soon as I can.

(SOFIA *watches as* EDWARD *exits the café. He stops in the
station entrance and looks back at her before heading out.*

23

SOFIA *runs out the back way and finds herself in a large corridor leading out to the taxi stand. She runs for the doors.* EDWARD *gets into a cab and sits there thinking.*
The DRIVER *waits for instructions, gets none, then looks back over his shoulder.*)
DRIVER: Where to, pal?

INT. GRAND CENTRAL STATION/STAIRS.

JAN *finishes scanning the café. He steps back over and meets* KURT *as he reaches the top of the stairs.* EDWARD *walks right by them and* JAN, *the older of the two, looks back over his shoulder. He hits* KURT *in the arm and they move off after* EDWARD.

INT. CAB. SAME TIME.

SOFIA *gets into the cab.*
SOFIA: Drive.
DRIVER: Where to?
SOFIA: Just drive.
DRIVER: Right.
     (*And he pulls out.*)

EXT. STATION. SAME TIME.

EDWARD *comes running back out into the street.* JAN *and* KURT *are hot on his trail.* KURT *catches up with him and throws him against the side of a car.*
SOFIA *looks on in horror as* . . .
EDWARD *swings his briefcase and tries to make another break for it.*
SOFIA *tries desperately to see as* . . .
KURT *tackles* EDWARD *in the middle of traffic.* JAN *violently pushes a curious bystander back.*
SOFIA *loses sight of it all through the traffic. Finally, she catches just a glimpse of* . . .
EDWARD *getting shoved into the car.* JAN *and* KURT *jump in themselves, and the car drives off.*
SOFIA, *concerned, looks on hopelessly as she is driven away.*
ISABELLE: (*Off*) 'In even the smallest things . . . She saw the pointlessness of hope . . . The impossibility of forgiveness.'

INT. GEORGE'S OFFICE. THAT AFTERNOON.

GEORGE, *the magazine editor, looks on, troubled, as* . . .

ISABELLE: (*Continues reading*) 'How is it possible, she asked,
that in a universe sustaining such conscientious brutality
. . . a friend can laugh, a mother smile, a father sacrifice,
or a lover kiss?
(*She looks up at* . . .
GEORGE. *He is concerned.*)

GEORGE: Is that it?

ISABELLE: Yes.
(*He looks away.*)

ISABELLE: (*Anxious*) What do you think?

GEORGE: (*Kindly*) Well, frankly, Isabelle, it's quite bad.

ISABELLE: It is?

GEORGE: I'm afraid so.

ISABELLE: But what's wrong with it?

GEORGE: It's not pornographic.

ISABELLE: (*Adamant*) Yes it is! (*Then, less certain* . . .) The first
part is!

GEORGE: It's poetry and don't you try and deny it!
(*She falls back, defeated.*)

ISABELLE: I'm sorry. I failed you.

(GEORGE *crosses to the window.*)

GEORGE: A mistake is not necessarily a failure, Isabelle.

ISABELLE: No?

(*He gets up and paces around the office.*)

GEORGE: Look at me. I'm a fairly successful editor of dirty
magazines. I never intended this. My aspiration was
defamatory journalism. My big ambition in life was to get
my hands on smutty pictures of the President's mistress. I
wanted to undermine huge corporations. Sow the seeds of
revolt by publishing the sordid details of high-level
government corruption. (*He sighs.*) But, you know, things
happen. (*He pushes a glass vase off the window sill.*) We drift
away from our vocation.

MOMENTS LATER.

GEORGE *is seated on the end of the couch, trying to console*
ISABELLE. *He reaches for his wallet.*

GEORGE: Now look, here's a hundred bucks. If you think up
something really dirty . . . really perverse . . . I mean,
really disgusting and gross . . . give me a call. OK?

ISABELLE: OK.

(*She hesitates, then takes the money.*)

EXT. PARK BENCH. AFTERNOON.

THOMAS *sits on a park bench.*
There's a twelve-year-old kid, SIMON, *sitting there reading* The Odyssey.

THOMAS: Hi.

SIMON: Hi.

THOMAS: What are you reading?

SIMON: *The Odyssey.*

THOMAS: Is it interesting?

SIMON: Sort of.

THOMAS: What's it about?

SIMON: Well, it's about this guy Odysseus mostly. He's King of this place called Ithaca. He's an OK guy. But he has to go and fight in this war and he's gone for ten years. And then, on the way back, he gets lost and he's wandering around for another ten years.

THOMAS: Wow.

SIMON: And he's got this really beautiful wife, Penelope, back home. All the other men in Ithaca wanna marry her.
(THOMAS *is engrossed.*)

THOMAS: Can I see it?
(SIMON *hands him the book.*)

SIMON: But Penelope doesn't want to marry any of them because she's waiting for Odysseus to get back. But, for all she knows, he could be dead.

THOMAS: Sounds great.
(THOMAS *hands it back.*)

SIMON: What are you reading?
(THOMAS *sees he means the magazine in his jacket pocket.*
THOMAS *pulls it out and hands it to* SIMON.)

THOMAS: 'Chicks.'
(SIMON *flips through the magazine with great interest.*
THOMAS *watches him, then . . .*)

THOMAS: Do you find those women attractive?

SIMON: I prefer girls my own age.

THOMAS: That's understandable.

SIMON: Do all women have hair between their legs like this?

THOMAS: Yeah. I guess. Most. There's a woman on page twenty-two who doesn't.

27

(SIMON *flips back to page twenty-two and checks this out.*)

SIMON: Can I keep this?

THOMAS: It belongs to a friend of mine. I gotta give it back.

SIMON: (*Turns page*) Look, a new Sofia Ludens movie!

    (THOMAS *looks on, alarmed by the reoccurrence of* SOFIA's *name.*)

THOMAS: Who?

SIMON: Sofia Ludens.

    (SIMON *shows him the page.*)

THOMAS: Who is it?

SIMON: She's the most notorious porno actress in the world. A friend of mine saw this movie in which . . .

    (*But he can't bring himself to say it out loud. He leans over and whispers to* THOMAS.)

INT. ABANDONED BUILDING, NEAR WATERFRONT.

JAN *and* KURT *toss* EDWARD *into a room.*

KURT: Kill him now or contact Frankfurt first?

JAN: Frankfurt?

KURT: Right?

JAN: Amsterdam.

KURT: You sure?

    (JAN *checks his notebook.*)

JAN: London.

KURT: (*Realizes*) Ah.

JAN: Tie him up.

    (KURT *does as he's told as . . .*

    JAN *moves to the window and flips open his cellular phone. He dials a number and has trouble getting a connection.*)

JAN: This thing is a piece of shit.

    (KURT *finishes with* EDWARD *and approaches with his own phone.*)

KURT: You should've gotten the one I got.

JAN: Which one is that?

KURT: DX 2047.

JAN: But that's what this one is.

KURT: No, look, that's a DX 2046. It's outdated.

JAN: It's brand new.

KURT: The technology improves daily.

JAN: How much you pay for that?

KURT: I lease it.

JAN: Really?

KURT: Yeah, works out cheaper in the long run.

    (JAN *puts his phone away and glances over at* EDWARD.)

JAN: Bring me that lamp.

KURT: Right.

    (KURT *brings him a busted lamp that lies near the door.*
    Keeping his eyes on EDWARD, JAN *cuts the cord off at the base*
    of the lamp. He holds up the split wires and sees that the copper
    at the end of each is exposed.

    KURT *plugs the cord into the wall socket, careful to keep the*
    exposed ends away from each other. He comes up behind
    EDWARD *and holds them inches away from either side of his*
    head.)

EDWARD: Jan, I don't have anything to do with Thomas
    anymore. I haven't seen him in over a year.

JAN: You know where Sofia is.

    (EDWARD *is taken off guard by this.*)

EDWARD: Sofia?

JAN: The girl. His wife?

    (EDWARD *pauses, then lies . . .*)

EDWARD: No. I don't. I don't know where she is.

(JAN *nods to* KURT *and he brings* . . .
The two exposed wires to EDWARD's *temples.*
ZAPPP!!!! EDWARD *jerks violently forward and* KURT *steps*
back.
JAN *waits.*)
JAN: Sofia Ludens.
EDWARD: What do you want with her? She doesn't know
  anything.
(JAN *nods to* KURT *again and* . . .
ZAPPP!!!!! *shocks* EDWARD *just a little longer than the last*
time. EDWARD *is stunned.* KURT *steps away from* EDWARD
and walks towards a window.)
EDWARD: Jan, look . . . we go way back. We were accountants
  together. You were a good accountant.
(JAN *looks out another window and sighs.*)
JAN: (*Unmoved*) I was younger then. I didn't know any better. I
  moved up. I'm more realistic now.
EDWARD: What if I told you Sofia killed Thomas.
JAN: I'd say you were lying.
EDWARD: But it's true.
JAN: Is it? Well, that's great. That's what we're here to find out.
  But first I've got to know where this girl Sofia is.
EDWARD: I won't tell you anything.

30

JAN: Do you realize we're going to torture you?

EDWARD: I won't tell you anything about Sofia.

JAN: (*To* KURT) He's a martyr.

KURT: Hopeless romantic.

JAN: Give me your phone.

> (*He takes* KURT's *phone, steps away, dials, listens, and has
> trouble with this one too.*)

JAN: This is just as bad as mine.

KURT: What?

> (KURT *takes it and dials, then* . . .)

KURT: Batteries must be low.

JAN: I'm gonna go down to the street and make some calls. See
what you can get out of him.

KURT: Right.

> (JAN *leaves.*
> *Close up:* EDWARD's *foot against the leg of the chair. It tenses
> up and trembles as he receives another long shock* . . .
> *Dissolve to:*)

EXT. ISABELLE'S/SIDEWALK. EARLY EVENING.

THOMAS *is waiting for* ISABELLE. *When she arrives, she's clearly
depressed.* THOMAS *is happy to see her and excited.*

31

THOMAS: Hi!

ISABELLE: Hello.

(She gets her mail and THOMAS *sees she's down.)*

THOMAS: What's wrong?

ISABELLE: I'm mediocre.

(ISABELLE *riffles through her mail, finds nothing important, and throws it back down.)*

THOMAS: You are, huh?

ISABELLE: I am. And I'm not sensual.

(ISABELLE *sits on the steps.)*

THOMAS: No. You're definitely sensual.

ISABELLE: I'm coldly intellectual. Too pale. Altogether too ethereal. And my feet hurt from wearing these stupid shoes.

(She rubs her foot.)

THOMAS: You wanna make love?

ISABELLE: No. Not now. Not yet. I'm tired and aggravated.

THOMAS: I'd like to rent a movie.

ISABELLE: A dirty movie?

THOMAS: Well, uh . . . Yeah.

(She hesitates, then shrugs and opens her purse . . .)

ISABELLE: OK. This is my membership card for the video store. It's over there by where the white supremacists hang out.

EXT. PIZZA PARLOR, PHONE BOOTH. EARLY EVENING.

JAN *is still talking on the phone as* . . .
KURT *approaches.* JAN *puts down the phone.*
JAN: How's it going?
KURT: He's had it.
JAN: Did you get anything out of him?
KURT: Address downtown. Tribeca.
   (*He hands a slip of paper to* JAN *who looks it over, before putting it in his pocket.*)
KURT: I'm gonna get something to eat.
JAN: Get a receipt.
KURT: Right.
   (JAN *picks up the phone again and* KURT *enters the pizza parlor, pushing a customer out of the way.*)

INT. ABANDONED BUILDING. EVENING.

A pair of squatters, TED *and* NICOLA, *enter the abandoned building.*
NICOLA: Where is it?
TED: Back here.
NICOLA: Oh, look at the water.
TED: That's the Hudson. That's New Jersey over there.
NICOLA: No way!
TED: Yeah.
NICOLA: This your lamp?
TED: You like it?
NICOLA: It's got no plug.
TED: Hey!
   (TED *walks toward the lamp as* NICOLA *wanders off screen.*)
NICOLA: I like the breeze. You told me New York wasn't gonna
   be as hot as Miami.
   (TED *picks up his lamp and inspects it.*)
TED: Fuck! Someone's tampered with my lamp!
NICOLA: There's a dead man in the corner.
   (*He turns and looks at her, scared.*)
TED: Bullshit.
   (NICOLA *comes back across to* TED.)
NICOLA: There is. He's got a chair tied to his foot.

33

INT. VIDEO STORE. SAME TIME.

THOMAS *finds the tape he's looking for and grabs it from the shelf.
The* CLERK *comes up behind him.*
THOMAS: You work here?
CLERK: Yeah.
THOMAS: I'd like to rent this tape.
  (THOMAS *hands the tape to the* CLERK.)
CLERK: Sofia Ludens, huh?
THOMAS: You know it?
CLERK: You can get arrested for watching this stuff.
THOMAS: Yeah?
CLERK: No.
  (THOMAS *grabs the box from the* CLERK *and walks to the next
  aisle.*)
CLERK: You're a pretty naïve guy, huh?
THOMAS: I've got amnesia.
CLERK: Drag. (*Then, back to business . . .*) You a member?
THOMAS: No. But a friend of mine is.
  (*And he hands the* CLERK *the card.*)
CLERK: Isabelle. She comes in here all the time.
THOMAS: She does, huh?
  (THOMAS *walks back to the first aisle.*)
CLERK: I didn't mean anything by that.
THOMAS: Good.
  (*He hands the box to the* CLERK.)

INT. ABANDONED BUILDING. LATER.

EDWARD *is battered, broken, and lifeless. His head is resting in*
NICOLA's *lap, while* TED *pours a cap full of whiskey from his pint.*
NICOLA: We should give him some water, don't you think?
TED: We don't have any water.
NICOLA: I need to take a shower, Ted.
TED: Lift his head a little.
  (*She does this and* TED *carefully pours the whiskey into*
  EDWARD's *mouth.*
  Nothing happens.
  They watch and wait.
  EDWARD *remains unconscious.*)

34

NICOLA: Give him some more.

    (TED *complies. This time, though,* EDWARD *coughs and lifts his head out of* NICOLA's *lap.*)

TED: (*Proud*) See, it works!

NICOLA: (*Of whiskey*) Gimme some.

TED: It's all we got.

NICOLA: (*Drinks, looks around*) This place ain't so bad.

INT. SAME PLACE. LATER.

EDWARD *is awake. He sits hunched like an animal in the corner, staring warily at . . .*

TED *and* NICOLA, *who are leaning against the far wall with their lamp and bundles.*

NICOLA: Do you think he's dangerous?

TED: Could be. I got my knife ready in case he does anything weird.

    (*And he shows her his pocket knife.*)

NICOLA: Maybe he's rabid.

TED: Rabid?

NICOLA: Yeah, you know, like when somebody has rabies.

TED: Could be. Could be he got bit by a rat.

NICOLA: Are there rats in here?

TED: Rats with rabies?

NICOLA: God, I hope not.

(EDWARD *continues to stare at them.*)

EXT. DOCK OUTSIDE ABANDONED BUILDING. NIGHT.

EDWARD *scrambles to his feet. He braces himself against the dock wall and stumbles along. He's 'shocked' and looks it. He's got a weirdly fierce, determined look in his eyes and his hair sticks straight out.*

TED *and* NICOLA *come out after him.* NICOLA *moves to help him up, but* TED *stops her.*

NICOLA: Honey, you be careful out there!

TED: Oh, Nicola, let him be. He's gotta learn to get along on his own.

NICOLA: I'm worried about him.

(*She tries to walk toward* EDWARD *as* TED *holds her back.*)

TED: Why are you worried about him? Come on, now. Why are you worried about that man? We gotta . . .

NICOLA: (*Calling to* EDWARD) Are you gonna be OK?

TED: Come on.

(*He drags her off as* EDWARD *stumbles along the wall.*)

INT. ISABELLE'S APT. NIGHT.

THOMAS *is sitting watching the videotape he has rented. We see* SOFIA *on the TV set and we hear a lot of panting and moaning and ferocious growling.*

ISABELLE *is sitting in the tub, reading from* The Life of Saint Teresa of Avila.

She pauses, considering what she had read.

THOMAS *is tilting his head back and forth, trying to figure out what's happening on screen.*

ISABELLE *listens to the tape, then . . .*

ISABELLE: What are you watching?

THOMAS: Something called 'Gang Rape'.

(THOMAS *picks up the remote control and pauses the TV.*
ISABELLE *appears wearing a robe.*
Startled, she walks toward the frozen image of SOFIA *on the TV. She stares at the TV and sits down.*

36

She stays there, staring at SOFIA, *till* THOMAS *comes back and sits beside her.*

THOMAS: *(Confused)* What is it?

ISABELLE: I know this girl.

THOMAS: It's Sofia Ludens.

ISABELLE: You know her?

THOMAS: No.

ISABELLE: How do you know her name?

THOMAS: It was written on the box.

> *(She watches him a moment longer, then looks back at the TV, intrigued.)*

ISABELLE: Why did you get this tape?

THOMAS: I was curious about the name Sofia.

ISABELLE: But you don't recognize her?

THOMAS: No.

> *(*ISABELLE *looks back at the screen. She reaches out and touches . . . The image of* SOFIA'*s face.)*

INT. SAME PLACE. LATER.

ISABELLE *is standing in the bathroom, concentrating. Finally . . .*

ISABELLE: This is it.

THOMAS: This is what?

ISABELLE: This is the thing I'm supposed to do.

THOMAS: I'm not sure I understand.

ISABELLE: This is it. This is the sign. This girl.

THOMAS: Are you sure? How can you tell?

ISABELLE: I just know. I can see it. It's in her face. (*Looks at him.*) And you're part of it.

THOMAS: (*Watches her, then*) How can I possibly be part of it?

ISABELLE: You have to be. Why else would you have come to me?

THOMAS: I didn't come to you. *You* found *me.*

ISABELLE: Yes. I found you. But you've brought me the sign.

THOMAS: How do you know it's a sign?

ISABELLE: Because I do.

(THOMAS, *anxious but skeptical, looks at the TV screen.*)

THOMAS: You could've gotten this sign yourself by going over to the video store.

ISABELLE: Yes. But I didn't. You did.

(THOMAS *is at a loss. He sighs and considers.* ISABELLE *watches him anxiously, then . . .*)

THOMAS: You think God wants you to find this girl?

ISABELLE: She's in trouble. I'm certain of it.

THOMAS: And what are you gonna do about that?
ISABELLE: (*Stops, pauses, weakens*) I don't know.
(THOMAS *looks back at* SOFIA's *face on the TV screen.*)

INT. PIZZA PARLOR. NIGHT.

EDWARD *moves down the sidewalk with dangerous intensity then
storms into a brightly lit pizza place.*
*He steps in and looks around before walking right in behind the
counter and grabbing a slice. As the pizza guy approaches him,*
EDWARD *steals the cigarette from his mouth, then shoves him out of
the way.*
EDWARD *wolfs down half a slice and drops it on the counter as he
moves ferociously towards the soda machine.*
The pizza guy staggers up and runs away.
EDWARD *pushes his face up under the soda machine, pushing the
lever that releases the soda with his chin. A steady stream of soda
begins pouring out and he drinks greedily.*

EXT. STREETS. NIGHT.

THOMAS *and* ISABELLE *come into the street and pass into
another* . . .
She strides out in front. THOMAS *looks all around, trying to
recognize things.*
THOMAS: (*Stops*) Where are we now?
ISABELLE: The coffee shop is up that way.
THOMAS: Sixth Avenue?
ISABELLE: Back there.
THOMAS: (*Figuring*) The water's that way, right?
ISABELLE: Yeah. But there is water that way, too.
(*He pauses, looks around, and shrugs.*)
THOMAS: It was a street with cobblestones. I remember seeing
the blood on the cobblestones.

EXT. COBBLESTONE STREET. MOMENTS LATER.

THOMAS *walks up and stops at the place where we saw him first.*
ISABELLE *joins him.*
THOMAS: This is it.

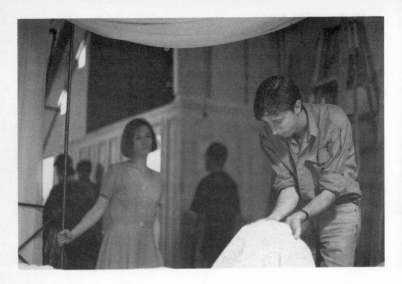

ISABELLE: Are you sure?
THOMAS: Yes. I remember.
(ISABELLE *kneels and looks at the ground.*)
ISABELLE: There is glass all over.
(THOMAS *gets down with her and sees . . .*
Shattered glass across the paving stones.
ISABELLE *and he both look up at the face of the building*
before them and see . . .
A large set of double windows on the second floor swinging open
and shut in the breeze. The glass is busted and the loft space
within seems dark and empty.)

INT. LOFT. A LITTLE LATER. NIGHT.

THOMAS *and* ISABELLE *cautiously walk in and sense the place is*
empty. It's a large loft and it is only partially renovated. There are
still tools and supplies lying around.
THOMAS: (*Hands back her hair pin*) Here.
ISABELLE: You did that pretty good.
THOMAS: What?
ISABELLE: Picking the lock.
THOMAS: It was easy.
ISABELLE: Maybe you're a locksmith.

40

(*The loft is just barely furnished. No one lives here very often.
They begin poking around.* THOMAS *approaches the open
window and looks out.*

ISABELLE *investigates what appears to be a bedroom. She
looks at the unmade bed and pauses, before coming down over
it and touching the sheets.*

She then sees . . .

An open armoir.

*She approaches and finds some articles of clothing in it. There
is, she finds, a bunch of stuff. Sexy lingerie, expensive dresses,
and shoes. She goes through it all.*

Meanwhile, THOMAS *finishes looking for clues at the window.
He comes back into the room and rummages through some
garbage on a table by the wall. An empty cigarette box,
matches, a straight-edge razor blade, two floppy disks and a
polaroid snapshot.*

*He lifts the snapshot into a shaft of light and winces in
disgust . . .*)

THOMAS: (*Quietly*) Shit!

(THOMAS *comes to the bedroom, deeply preoccupied. He stops
in the doorway, though, when he sees . . .*

ISABELLE *dressed in a short skirt, high heels and expensive
lingerie.*

41

He is surprised.
ISABELLE *is uncertain of the effect.*
THOMAS *and* ISABELLE *come closer to each other.*)
ISABELLE: What is it?
(THOMAS, *disturbed, looks her straight in the eye.*)
THOMAS: Do you still hope I don't find out who I am?
(*She pauses and looks away, sadly.*)
ISABELLE: It doesn't matter to me who you were.
(*As she looks back up at him, he comes closer and lets her hair down.*
Dissolve to:
THOMAS *and* ISABELLE *are now lying together on the bed.*)
ISABELLE: You're not remembering anything, are you?
THOMAS: No. I don't remember anything.
ISABELLE: I'm afraid.
THOMAS: Of what?
ISABELLE: I'm afraid I won't know how.
THOMAS: How to what?
ISABELLE: Make love.
THOMAS: Don't worry.
ISABELLE: Maybe I won't like it.
(THOMAS *pauses then kisses her lips lightly.*)
THOMAS: Do you like that?
ISABELLE: Yes.
(*He kisses her on the shoulder.*)
THOMAS: Like that?
ISABELLE: Yes. I like that.
(*He moves his face down her body and* ISABELLE *sighs deeply as we see . . .*
Her clothes strewn on the ground beyond the bed.)
THOMAS: You like that?
ISABELLE: I like that especially.
(*She moans blissfully.*)
ISABELLE: Keep doing that.
THOMAS: What?
ISABELLE: That.
THOMAS: You mean this?
(*And he does something to her.*)
ISABELLE: Ohhhh!!!!
(*But then . . .*

42

They stop and look up.)
ISABELLE: What is that?
THOMAS: What?
ISABELLE: Listen.
    (*And they now hear the front door opening.*
    At the door: JAN *and* KURT *enter. They pause and listen.*
    Nothing.
    They come in and close the door.)
JAN: Go check the bedroom. I'll find the lights.
    (*They fan out into the loft.*
    KURT *comes to the bedroom doorway and looks in.*
    Nothing.
    He goes back out.
    In the main room: JAN *goes through the junk on the table just*
    as THOMAS *did. He finds the floppy disks and lifts them. But*
    then . . .
    JAN *hears someone in the hall.*)

INT. STAIRWELL. SAME TIME.

SOFIA *comes in the front door, looking back into the street, trying not*
to let anyone see her. She starts up the stairs.

INT. LOFT. SAME TIME.

JAN *ducks into the shadows as . . .*
KURT *steps behind the door.*
ISABELLE *and* THOMAS, *hiding in the armoir, listen and wonder.*
The door opens and SOFIA *creeps in. She quietly closes the door*
behind her and comes face to face with . . .
KURT.
Her mouth falls open but she can't scream.
KURT *falls on her and covers her mouth. Now, she starts kicking*
and screaming.
KURT *holds her back for* JAN *to see.*
JAN: (*Off*) Yeah, that's her.
KURT: Should I break her neck?
JAN: No. I wanna talk to her.

43

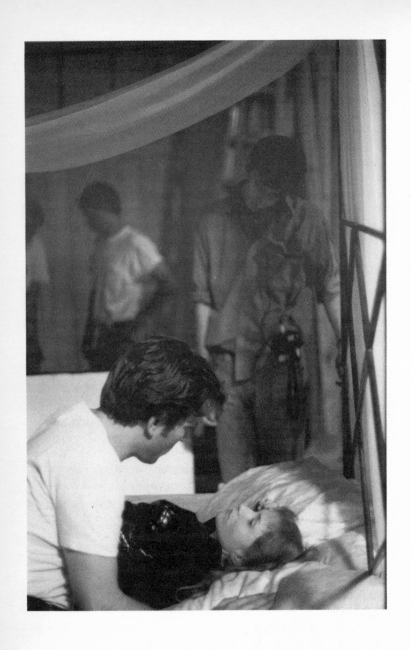

EXT. PHONE BOOTH/STREET. SAME TIME.

A harried YOUNG MOTHER *is on the phone, while her two little kids run around nearby.*

MOTHER (*Hysterical*) I swear to God, you'll read about it in the newspapers tomorrow, Joey! I swear to God, I . . .
(EDWARD *strides up and tosses her out of his way, grasping the receiver as . . .*
The MOTHER *comes back at him, irate.*)

MOTHER: What the fuck is your problem, pal!
(EDWARD *reaches out and grabs her pocket book.*
She tries to take it from him.)

MOTHER: Give it to me!
(EDWARD *punches her hard in the stomach and she falls back. He goes through the purse, dumping everything out till he finds some change.*
The MOTHER *runs away screaming for help . . .*)

MOTHER: Police! Goddammit, Police!
(*Meanwhile, the kids spray* EDWARD *with their water guns. But the phone eats his quarter and still doesn't work, so he starts punching the shit out of it. He manages to rip the phone right out of the booth.*
Then the POLICE *show up.*)

POLICEMAN: (*Tackling* EDWARD) All right, all right, Sir. Calm down.
(*He manages to bring* EDWARD *to the ground as the* MOTHER *runs around hysterically, kicking him.*)

POLICEMAN: All right! Hey, lady, back off! Back off.
(*A* SECOND POLICEMAN *pushes her away.*)

SECOND POLICEMAN: Take it easy. Now, take it easy.

MOTHER: Let me go. (*She wrestles free.*) Where are my kids? You goddamn son of a bitch! Where are my kids?

INT. LOFT. LATER.

SOFIA *kneels on the floor as* KURT *fastens her hands behind her back to a column.*
JAN *comes over with the floppy disks.*
JAN: Sofia, my name's Jan. I work for Mister Jacques.
SOFIA: I hate you. I hate Jacques. I hate everybody.

45

JAN: Of course. It's a rough time to be a human being. Here, sit
up.
  (*They sit her up.*)
SOFIA: What did you do to Edward?
JAN: Edward's dead.
  (*She weakens and hangs her head.*
  They wait. Then . . .)
JAN: Let's talk about these floppy disks.
  (*She doesn't respond.*
  JAN *grabs her by the hair.*)
JAN: Hey!
SOFIA: Why did you have to do that? He wasn't a danger to
you.
  (JAN, *at a loss, looks at* KURT.)
JAN: What's she talking about?
KURT: She's upset about the accountant.
  (JAN *realizes, then returns to* SOFIA.)
JAN: Look, forget about Edward. Now, I wanna know about
these floppy disks. Where'd you get them?
  (*She grudgingly responds . . .*)
SOFIA: From Thomas.
JAN: When?
SOFIA: He had them with him yesterday.

JAN: He's here in New York?

SOFIA: He's dead.

JAN: Tell the truth.

SOFIA: That is the truth! I pushed him out that window!
> (JAN *looks at* KURT. *They both look over at the window.*
> KURT *shakes his head.*)

KURT: Makes no sense, Jan.

JAN: Edward said the same thing.

KURT: It would've been in the papers. We would've heard.
> (JAN *considers his options, then looks back at* SOFIA.)

JAN: Sofia, look, you're gonna have to tell us everything you
know about Thomas.

SOFIA: But what can I tell you?

JAN: Why is he in New York.

SOFIA: But he's dead!

JAN: Is this where he lives?

SOFIA: (*Indignant*) This is *my* place! I paid the rent with my *own*
money!

KURT: It's a dump.

SOFIA: (*Hurt*) I was having it fixed up. I bought some furniture,
but I ran out of money.

KURT: Typical.

JAN: (*Annoyed*) Kurt, please.

KURT: (*Lays off*) Right.
> (THOMAS, *now out of the armoir, listens intently from the*
> *bedroom.*)

JAN: Sofia, who has Thomas been in contact with?

SOFIA: I don't know.

JAN: How long has he been in the States?

SOFIA: Please! I hate him just as much as you do! I don't know
anything!
> (JAN *and* KURT *sit back and size up the situation.*)

JAN: What do you think, Kurt?

KURT: (*Professionally*) We could perform a water torture in the
bathroom but that could be noisy. (*Looks around, considers*
then shrugs.) There are things I can do with a pair of pliers.

JAN: Do you need me for anything?

KURT: No.

JAN: Good. I'm gonna check out these disks.
> (*And after a brief pause, he leaves to go down to the car.*)

47

INT. POLICE PRECINCT. NIGHT.

The cops handcuff EDWARD *to a seat at the end of* OFFICER
MELVILLE'*s desk.*
She sits, looking at him, obviously and immediately smitten with this
dangerous and strange man.
EDWARD *hangs there in the chair and looks back at her wildly.*
OFFICER MELVILLE: Hi. I'm Officer Melville. You can call me
　　Patsy. (*No response, she continues, shyly* . . .) They send
　　people to me when they have no identification. Sometimes
　　they don't even know their own name. (*Looks down,*
　　sadly . . .) I find that so incredibly sad. (*She reaches out and*
　　touches his hand.) Do you understand me?
　　(*He is looking at her hand on his.*
　　She sees this. She removes it.
　　He looks up to her face.)
　　Can you hear what I'm saying?
　　(*But he just looks past her and stares at the wall, abstracted.*
　　OFFICER MELVILLE *sighs and looks down at her desk.*)
　　God, I can't take this job.
DETECTIVE: You gotta toughen yourself up, Melville!
OFFICER MELVILLE: (*Angry*) What do I have to do, become
　　completely insensitive!?

DETECTIVE: Just do your job.
> (*She heaves a tremendously tortured and world-weary sigh, then manages to lift her head and look at . . .*
> EDWARD, *who is intently focused on something behind her.*
> OFFICER MELVILLE *follows his gaze to . . .*
> *The polaroid of* THOMAS.
> *She looks back at* EDWARD. *He is transfixed by the polaroid. Turning back, she removes the photo from the wall, and brings it back to the desk. She looks at it herself for a moment, then shows it to* EDWARD.)

OFFICER MELVILLE: Is this a friend of yours?
> (*Scared,* EDWARD *shakes his head, 'no'.*
> OFFICER MELVILLE *looks back at the photo, considers things, then hazards another guess.*)

OFFICER MELVILLE: (*Horrified*) Did this man harm you in some way?
> (EDWARD *pauses, then nods his head, 'yes'.*
> OFFICER MELVILLE *sighs again and rests her head in her hands.*)

INT. LOFT. NIGHT.

KURT *removes his holster and hangs it up. He then approaches*
SOFIA, *who is still tied up.*

KURT: Can I ask you a personal question?

SOFIA: Leave me alone.

KURT: Do you resent your position as a woman in the motion picture industry? I'm sorry. I find you very attractive, and I'm interested in commodities.

SOFIA: What are you talking about?
> (*He places a pair of pliers on the floor and starts untying her shoe.*)

KURT: A commodity is an article of trade. A product in the purest sense.

SOFIA: What has this got to do with me?

KURT: You're a product.

SOFIA: I am?

KURT: You're a commodity. Thomas tendered your body in exchange for money.

SOFIA: So I'm an article of trade?

KURT: Yes. A useful thing, in terms of classic capitalism. I studied economics. I know what I'm talking about.
(THOMAS *and* ISABELLE *search for weapons. They find a power drill and* THOMAS *plugs it in.*)
KURT: (*To* SOFIA) I want you to tell me why Thomas was in New York and who he had come to see.
(SOFIA *is trembling.*)
SOFIA: He came to see me.
KURT: Why would he come to see you?
SOFIA: He wanted me back.
KURT: He wanted you back?
SOFIA: I ran away.
KURT: From Thomas?
SOFIA: (*Desperate*) He loved me.
KURT: And you had left him?
SOFIA: Yes.
KURT: Why had you left him?
SOFIA: He scared me!
KURT: But you just told me that he loved you?
(SOFIA *falls back, exhausted.*)
SOFIA: I just want to change my life.
KURT: What about Thomas?
SOFIA: He took advantage of me.
KURT: Whose fault is that?
SOFIA: I killed him! I did! I swear!
KURT: I don't believe you.
SOFIA: Please don't hurt me!
(*He shoves the rag in her mouth.*)
KURT: Why would you be scared of a man who loved you?
(*WHIRRRR!!!!! He and* SOFIA *look up and see . . .*
ISABELLE *gunning the power drill. She stands in the middle of the room; a drop-dead sexy woman with high heels and a power tool.*)
KURT: (*Amazed*) Wow!
(THOMAS *takes* KURT's *gun out of the holster. Both armed,* THOMAS *and* ISABELLE *pursue* KURT *with their weapons. They corner him and send him falling out the window. Silence.*)

EXT. COBBLESTONE STREET. SAME TIME.

JAN, *at the car, about to slip the disks into a lap-top of his own, hears . . .*
KURT *hit the ground with a thud.*
He leans out and sees . . .
KURT *lying there in the street.*
He pauses, incredulous, then gets out, tosses the computer and disks in the car, and approaches KURT.

INT. LOFT. SAME TIME.

THOMAS *and* ISABELLE *look blankly at the open window, shocked.*
SOFIA, *too, stares, amazed.*

EXT. STREET.

JAN *comes down over* KURT, *sees he's dead, and looks up at the loft.*

INT. LOFT.

ISABELLE *and* THOMAS *are about to leave when* ISABELLE *notices* SOFIA *crouched motionless on the floor. She comes back and urges the girl to come with them.*
Together, they clamber into the elevator.

EXT. STAIRWELL. SAME TIME.

With his gun drawn, JAN *stealthily makes his way into the building from the street.*

EXT. ALLEY/STREET. SAME TIME.

THOMAS, ISABELLE, *and* SOFIA *creep out of a side door that leads to the alley. They make their way up the alley and into the street, where they see . . .*
JAN'S *car.*
They check the street, then run for the car.
THOMAS *opens the car door and waits as . . .*
ISABELLE *runs across the street, but stops and turns to find . . .*

SOFIA *hesitating in the street, looking at* THOMAS, *scared.*
THOMAS *and* ISABELLE *exchange looks, then* ISABELLE *returns to*
SOFIA . . .
ISABELLE: It's OK.
>   (SOFIA *is not so sure. She stays where she is.*)

INT. LOFT. SAME TIME.

JAN *enters. He looks around.*
Nothing.
Then he hears, in the street, the car pulling away.
He runs to the window and looks out as . . .

EXT. STREET. SAME TIME.

The car screeches around the corner and disappears.

INT. LOFT. SAME TIME.

JAN *throws up his hands, beaten.*
JAN: Fuck!
>   (*He stands there shaking his head when he sees . . .*
>   SOFIA's *bag on the floor.*
>   *He comes over and picks it up. As he does, her change purse*
>   *falls out of it. He lifts this, opens it, and finds . . .*
>   *The address* EDWARD *gave her of the house in Portchester.*

INT. CAR. A LITTLE LATER.

THOMAS *is driving fast and recklessly.*
ISABELLE: Let me drive.
THOMAS: Why?
ISABELLE: Because you don't know how.
THOMAS: I know how, I just can't remember.
ISABELLE: But it's the same thing.
>   (THOMAS, *unsettled, looks back at . . .*
>   SOFIA, *who watches him, terrified.*)
THOMAS: What's the matter with her, anyway?
ISABELLE: She's afraid of you.
THOMAS: Great! What are we gonna do now?

ISABELLE: Let me drive.
THOMAS: No!
ISABELLE: Be careful.
SOFIA: Go north.
THOMAS: What?
SOFIA: Portchester.
　(*Dissolve to:*)

INT. ROADSIDE RESTAURANT. NIGHT.

THOMAS *is sitting by himself at the counter.*
ISABELLE *and* SOFIA *are at another table far across the restaurant.*
They just sit there silently. ISABELLE *looks over at* THOMAS.
ISABELLE *turns to* SOFIA.
SOFIA *is watching her.*
SOFIA: You're wearing my stuff.
　(ISABELLE *only then remembers her new clothes. She pauses,*
　then . . .)
ISABELLE: Sorry.
SOFIA: They look good on you.
ISABELLE: Thanks.
　(ISABELLE *takes this in, thinking.*
　SOFIA *watches her, then looks over again at* THOMAS.)

SOFIA: You're in love with him.

ISABELLE: I only just met him.

SOFIA: Is it true he can't remember his name?

ISABELLE: He has amnesia.

(SOFIA *thinks this through, then smokes and looks away.*)

SOFIA: I hate him anyway.

(ISABELLE *joins* THOMAS, *who is anxious for news.*)

THOMAS: What'd she say?

ISABELLE: She's in trouble with those men. She doesn't want to go to the police.

THOMAS: Does she know who I am?

ISABELLE: Yes. But she won't tell me.

(ISABELLE *watches him, pauses, then proceeds carefully . . .*)

ISABELLE: She said you're a very dangerous man. (*Pauses, then . . .*) I'll be outside.

(*He watches her go, not sure what to make of her reaction. He looks over at* SOFIA.

Moments later, SOFIA *watches as* THOMAS *comes close. She is scared.*

He pauses near the table.)

THOMAS: Do you mind if I sit down?

(SOFIA *looks away.*

He sighs and sits down at the booth behind SOFIA.)

THOMAS: (*Frustrated*) Look, I can't remember anything. (*No response.*) I can't imagine what I've done to you. But I want you to know whatever it is I can do to help you, I will.

(*She betrays no emotion. Then she relaxes a little. She glances out at the parking lot.*)

SOFIA: This woman, Isabelle, who is she?

THOMAS: She helped me out.

SOFIA: She doesn't know who you are?

THOMAS: No. Neither do I.

SOFIA: (*Pauses, then*) But I do.

THOMAS: Will you tell me?

SOFIA: No. I won't.

(*She looks down, slides out from the booth and leaves.* THOMAS *watches her go, disappointed and angry.*)

EXT. HOUSE. LATER THAT NIGHT.

THOMAS, ISABELLE, *and* SOFIA *drive up and get out of the car.*
THOMAS: (*To* SOFIA) You got a key?
SOFIA: No.
> (THOMAS *moves toward the house and smashes a window.*)

INT. HOUSE. MOMENTS LATER.

They check the place out. Everyone is very tired.
ISABELLE: There is only one bed upstairs.
THOMAS: You get some sleep. I'll stay up. Give me the gun.
> (ISABELLE *does not budge. This makes* THOMAS *extremely impatient.*)
THOMAS: Give me the gun!
> (ISABELLE *hesitantly takes out the gun, hands it to* THOMAS, *then runs up the stairs.* SOFIA *follows.*
> THOMAS *is crushed. He watches them go and waits a few moments after the door is closed and locked before heaving a huge sigh and turning away.*)

INT. BEDROOM. MOMENTS LATER.

ISABELLE *sits on the edge of the bed. She's confused and sad.*
SOFIA *is lying on the bed behind* ISABELLE, *watching her.*
ISABELLE: Are you sure you don't want to go to the police?
SOFIA: They'll only send me back to Holland and Mister Jacques will have me killed when I get there.
ISABELLE: Who is Mister Jacques?
SOFIA: It doesn't matter.
ISABELLE: I know a place not far from here where you can hide for a while. You'll be safe.
SOFIA: I wish they'd just kill me.
ISABELLE: Don't talk like that.
> (SOFIA *looks at* ISABELLE. *She's terrified and childlike in her despair.*)
SOFIA: I'm not afraid of dying. I'm afraid of pain.
> (ISABELLE *moves closer.*)
ISABELLE: No one is going to hurt you.
SOFIA: Yesterday I thought I was so smart. Like I was going to

help people and stop bad things from happening. I was going to change things. Change my life. (*Pauses, then . . .*) I got a man killed.

INT. KITCHEN. MOMENTS LATER.

THOMAS *is sitting at the table with the gun pointed at his head.*
ISABELLE *comes out and grabs the gun.*
ISABELLE: Don't do that!
THOMAS: It's not loaded.
ISABELLE: I know. I emptied it. But who cares.
(*She returns it to her handbag.*)
THOMAS: (*Angry*) You gave me an unloaded gun to protect ourselves with.
ISABELLE: I was scared.
THOMAS: You don't trust me at all now, do you?
ISABELLE: I'm sorry.
THOMAS: Did you think I was gonna walk in there and shoot the two of you in your sleep!?
ISABELLE: She told me you had done things like that before.
(THOMAS *stops, speechless. He stares at her.*)
THOMAS: What else did she say?

56

ISABELLE: She said you were in trouble too.
   (*He looks up at her.*)
THOMAS: In trouble with who?
ISABELLE: Those men back there.
THOMAS: And who are they?
ISABELLE: (*Wearily*) They work for a highly respectable yet
   ultimately sinister international corporation with political
   connections.
   (THOMAS *gives her a sideways look.*)
THOMAS: Are you making this up?
ISABELLE: No. It's true.
   (*Moments later,* THOMAS *is pacing back and forth while*
   ISABELLE *tries to call up data from the floppy disks.*)
THOMAS: What do they want with me?
ISABELLE: They want to kill you.
THOMAS: Why?
ISABELLE: Because you know what's on these.
THOMAS: (*Takes one*) Yeah? What the fuck are these?
ISABELLE: Floppy disks.
THOMAS: Floppy what?
ISABELLE: (*Annoyed*) Disks!
THOMAS: But they're square.
ISABELLE: (*Concentrating*) SHHH!!!!!
THOMAS: (*To himself*) And they're not floppy either, they're
   stiff.
   (THOMAS *stops pacing and stares at* ISABELLE, *who has
   stopped typing.*)
THOMAS: (*Watches*) What is it?
   (*She stands and leans against him for comfort.*)
ISABELLE: This is it. Whatever it is I'm supposed to do, this is
   it.
   (THOMAS *holds her even tighter, then lets her go and sits down
   on the stairs.*)
THOMAS: Isabelle, I don't think this is divine intervention.
ISABELLE: You don't?
THOMAS: No. It's not a miracle. And it's not God's will. You
   know what I think this is? This – I think – is just really
   . . . bad . . . luck. And it's got nothing to do with you.
   (*She sits down beside him.*) So you shouldn't get anymore
   involved than you already are.

57

ISABELLE: (*Insists*) I know I was meant to find this girl and to help her.
(*She leans her head on his shoulder.*)
THOMAS: (*Stops, sighs*) You do, huh?
ISABELLE: Yes. I think maybe I'm supposed to save her from you.
(THOMAS *freezes and watches the back of her head, crushed.*)
THOMAS: I'm the same man you knew yesterday.
(*She doesn't respond. Then . . .*)
ISABELLE: Maybe.

INT. POLICE PRECINCT. DAWN.

EDWARD *is handcuffed to a bench in the hallway.*
OFFICER MELVILLE *joins him.*
OFFICER MELVILLE: We have no information on this man. He has no record. We've checked everything.
(EDWARD *throws his head back and growls, frustrated. He tugs at his hand-cuffs.*
OFFICER MELVILLE *falls back, looking on, crushed with pity. The* DETECTIVE *looks him up and down, disgusted.*)
DETECTIVE: The guy's a maniac, Melville. I can tell.
OFFICER MELVILLE: (*Indignant*) Sir, he's troubled.
DETECTIVE: He say anything yet?
OFFICER MELVILLE: (*Looks down*) No. Nothing.
(EDWARD *settles down and glares at the* DETECTIVE.)
DETECTIVE: Then get him outta here, Melville. He's a mental case.
(EDWARD *looks back at* OFFICER MELVILLE. *Then . . .*)
OFFICER MELVILLE: I'm sorry. I have to book you. But you get to make a phone call.

INT. HOUSE. MORNING.

The phone rings and THOMAS *wakes up from where he is sleeping on the floor.*
The phone keeps ringing. He hesitates, but then gets up and answers it.
THOMAS: (*Careful*) Hello?

INT. POLICE PRECINCT. SAME TIME.

EDWARD *looks at the receiver, stunned, and hangs up quick.*

INT. HOUSE. SAME TIME.

THOMAS *replaces the receiver, spooked. He sees . . .*
SOFIA *is still sound asleep in the next room. But* ISABELLE *is nowhere to be seen.*

INT. HOSPITAL. LATER.

EDWARD *sits brooding horribly amongst the confused, angry, and troubled misfits the city drags in off the streets each day.*
There is one armed guard at the entrance to the wide, nondescript and noisy detention center. OFFICER MELVILLE *signs some forms and exchanges a few words with the guard, pointing to . . .*
EDWARD, *who watches her without moving.*
She starts towards him.
She comes up before him and stops. With an infinitely kind and thoughtful expression, she undoes his handcuffs and reassures him.
OFFICER MELVILLE: Don't worry. Everything's going to be
    alright.
    (*He gazes into her eyes at length; calm, distant, and sad. She smiles. Then . . .*
    He grabs her by the neck and drags her to the ground.
    People start screaming and diving for cover as . . .
    He grabs her gun.
    The one guard comes running, drawing his gun, but . . .
    EDWARD *fires and . . .*
    The guard goes down.
    With the gun to her head, EDWARD *drags* OFFICER MELVILLE
    towards the doors.)

EXT. HOSPITAL. SAME TIME.

EDWARD *runs in front of a car and forces the driver out at gun point. He shoves* OFFICER MELVILLE *away and she falls in the street as he jumps in the car and speeds off.*

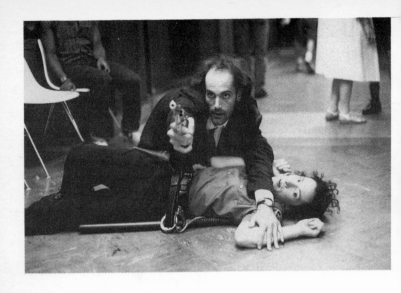

INT. HOSPITAL. MOMENTS LATER.

OFFICER MELVILLE *comes running in and jumps down upon . . .*
The guard who lies staring at the ceiling, scared to death and trying
to breath.

EXT. PHONEBOOTH, PORTCHESTER TRAIN STATION.

ISABELLE *is in a phone booth. A train is heard pulling in to the*
station overhead.

ISABELLE: Yes. George? I know it's early, but I have something
    interesting. No. It's not disgusting actually, but very
    damaging documentation of high-level government
    corruption. I don't know what government exactly. Maybe
    a few.
    (*Meanwhile,* JAN *steps down from the train platform, sees his*
    car, and looks over at ISABELLE.)
    OK. Look, George, I'm on the run from a group of
    bloodthirsty corporate assassins and I'm hiding in the
    country. Ummhum, OK. I'll call you when I can. Expect
    an envelope tomorrow. Bye.
    (*And she hangs up. She steps out of the booth, and drops the*

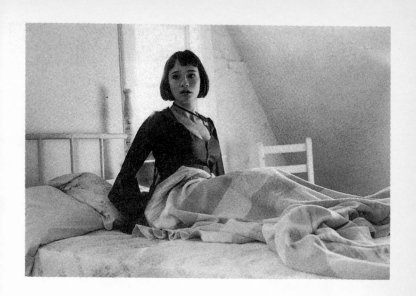

*envelope containing the floppy disks in a mailbox nearby
when . . .
A hand grabs her wrist.
She looks from her hand up to see . . .*
JAN.)

INT. HOUSE. MOMENTS LATER.

SOFIA *wakes. She lies there for a moment, then rolls over and
sees . . .*
THOMAS *at the window, looking out into the yard.*
SOFIA'*s mouth opens, but no words come out. She dares not move.*
THOMAS *pauses, then . . .*
THOMAS: Where's Isabelle?
SOFIA: (*Petrified*) I don't know.
THOMAS: The car's gone.
   (*He looks back in at her, hoping she's got some idea.
   She just stares at him.
   He shakes his head, frustrated.*)
THOMAS: Look, I'm not going to hurt you. Relax.
   (*But she doesn't. She just steps further away.
   Annoyed,* THOMAS *sighs, then . . .*

The phone rings again. He stops, pauses, then looks at SOFIA.
She looks off at it as well, anxious.)

THOMAS: It rang before too.

SOFIA: Did you answer it?

(*He shrugs, uncertain if he should have . . .*)

THOMAS: Well . . . yes.

(*The phone keeps ringing and . . .*)

SOFIA: (*Rolls her eyes*) Why?

THOMAS: I thought it might be Isabelle.

SOFIA: (*sighs*) You idiot! They probably know where we are now!

THOMAS: Well, how was I supposed to know?

SOFIA: How were you supposed to know! You *used* to know everything!

(*He throws up his arms . . .*)

THOMAS: (*angry*) Oh yeah! Well why don't you tell me *what* I *used* to know!

(SOFIA *catches herself, then turns away in a huff.*)

SOFIA: Why don't you just go and answer the phone!

THOMAS: Fuck you!

SOFIA: Drop dead!

THOMAS: Listen, you! I've had about enough of this shit! Are you gonna tell me who I am and what's going on around here or what!

(*The phone keeps ringing . . .*)

SOFIA: (*Spiteful*) You want to know who you are?

THOMAS: Yes!

SOFIA: Why should I tell you who you are?

THOMAS: Because I'm asking you to!

SOFIA: And I'm supposed to do whatever you want me to do, is that it!

(*He turns and walks away . . .*)

THOMAS: Forget it! I don't care! I don't want to know!

SOFIA: (*Stomps her foot*) Now, you see, that's just like you!

(*He spins back, wild . . .*)

THOMAS: *What* is!

(*She turns away, victorious.*)

SOFIA: Answer the phone!

THOMAS: You answer the goddamn phone!

(*And he storms down the stairs.*
SOFIA, *left there alone, listens as the phone rings and rings and*

rings. Finally, she goes out to the hall, hesitates, but then answers it.)

SOFIA: (*Cautious*) Hello?

JAN: (*off*) Sofia, it's Jan.

(*Her mouth falls open and she'd scream if she could, but she's too scared.*)

I've got Isabelle and I know where you are. Now I'm going to make you a deal. You tell me if Thomas is with you; just answer yes, and you and Isabelle won't be harmed. But if you say no . . . Isabelle's dead.

(*She nearly faints at this, but holds the wall.*)

Yes or no. Is he with you? If he is, there'll be a knock at the door in five minutes. Let him answer it.

(*She swallows and attempts to speak, but can only catch her breath.*)

Yes . . . or . . . no? Yes: and you and Isabelle are free. No: and Isabelle is dead.

(*She looks down to . . .*

THOMAS, *who is standing at the bottom of the stairs.*

She stands there as if hung by wires, her lip trembling, her face pale.)

JAN: (*Off*) Sofia, yes . . . or . . . no?

(THOMAS *waits, watching her.*

She looks away, finally, and stares at the wall. Then, weakly . . .)

SOFIA: Yes.

(*Click.* JAN *hangs up.*

SOFIA *is awe-struck. She lowers the receiver slowly but still holds onto it, as if for support. She gazes down the stairs at* THOMAS. THOMAS *takes a step closer, concerned . . .*)

THOMAS: Are you OK?

(*She passes out, and collapses.* THOMAS *runs up and comes down over her.*

But then he hears a car pull up outside.

He looks up, startled, uncertain of what to do.

He lifts SOFIA *off the floor and carries her into the bedroom just as . . .*

CRASH!!!! The front door is kicked in.

It's EDWARD. *He stands there in the doorway with his stolen gun. He pauses, listens, hears nothing, then steps in.*

63

He comes up the stairs and finds SOFIA *in bed, asleep.*
He prowls around the upstairs rooms, sensing someone is there.
THOMAS *is hiding in the bathroom. He looks around for a*
weapon and finds a rusty old razor blade.
Finally, EDWARD *roams back into the bedroom.*
SOFIA *stirs, groggy and confused. She rolls her head to one side*
and sees . . .
EDWARD *lean his head in the doorway and check on her.*
She goes completely still. She blinks.
EDWARD *raises a finger to his lips, signalling her to keep quiet,*
then steps back out.
SOFIA *pauses, amazed, and leans up on her elbow.*
As EDWARD *steps into the hallway,* THOMAS *steps up behind*
him and . . .
Holds the razor to his throat just as EDWARD *puts the gun to*
THOMAS*'s head.*
They remain there, close and still, neither one able or willing to
move, as . . .
SOFIA *emerges quietly from the bedroom.*
THOMAS *and* EDWARD *both look at her.*
SOFIA*'s face lights up and all the cares in the world are*
suddenly thrown right out the window as she exclaims . . .)

SOFIA: Oh, Edward! You're alive!
(But the front door is thrown open and . . .
JAN *enters, takes aim and . . .*
BOOM!!!! SOFIA *is thrown against the wall, shot in the*
shoulder.
EDWARD *swings out and shoots . . .*
Catching JAN *in the chest and throwing him back out of the*
house as ISABELLE *stumbles in.*
THOMAS *falls down over* SOFIA *to see if she's breathing as*
EDWARD *runs down the stairs, past* ISABELLE, *and out of the*
house.)

EXT. FIELD. MOMENTS LATER.

EDWARD *runs out of the house and shoots* JAN *repeatedly.* JAN,
though, continues stumbling along before finally collapsing face down
in the grass. All his bullets gone, EDWARD *drops his gun and just*
stands there, looking around, with nothing to do.

EXT. HOUSE. MOMENTS LATER.

THOMAS *carries* SOFIA *to the car as* ISABELLE *guides* EDWARD, *who is completely stunned, over to the car. She forces him in and helps* THOMAS *with* SOFIA. *Finally . . .*
THOMAS: Let me drive.
ISABELLE: No, no.
   (*She gets into the driver's seat.*)

EXT. FIELD. TWENTY MINUTES LATER.

The DECTECTIVE *finishes taking a look at* JAN's *body, then waves for the ambulance people to take him away.*
A YOUNGER DETECTIVE *steps up holding* OFFICER MELVILLE's *gun in a plastic bag.*
YOUNGER DETECTIVE: It is Melville's gun, sir.
DETECTIVE: Have we got a trace on the car?
YOUNGER DETECTIVE: It's been spotted. There's an officer in
   pursuit.
DETECTIVE: (*Walks away*) Where?
YOUNGER DETECTIVE: (*Follows*) About five miles away, headed
   east, toward the river.
DETECTIVE: Anything in that direction?
YOUNGER DETECTIVE: Yes sir. A convent.

EXT. CONVENT. SAME TIME.

ISABELLE *knocks on the front door of the convent.*
Momentarily, a nun, SISTER AMELIA, *appears. She sees them and steps out, looking down at the wounded girl. Then she looks at* ISABELLE.
AMELIA: Isabelle?

INT. CONVENT. MOMENTS LATER.

They all rush in and are met by a few more nuns who lead them to the infirmary.

INT. INFIRMARY. MOMENTS LATER.

THOMAS *sets* SOFIA *down and the nuns take over.*
The Mother Superior, SISTER CELESTINE, *shoves* THOMAS *out of the way and examines the wounds. She sighs and tisks grumpily.*
CELESTINE: This is bad. (*Leans back, sees* THOMAS *again, then to* ISABELLE.) Who's he?
ISABELLE: He's my friend.
(*The older nun looks back at* THOMAS.)
CELESTINE: Tell him to wait outside.
(THOMAS *moves off, reluctantly.*)
CELESTINE: Isabelle, are you in trouble?
ISABELLE: (*Gulps*) Yes.
(SISTER CELESTINE *watches her a moment, considering, then picks up a towel.*)
CELESTINE: I knew you'd get into trouble. I knew it. (*She sits.*) You should have never left here! Never!
(ISABELLE *doesn't argue.* SOFIA *reaches up and touches her arm.*
ISABELLE *stops and watches as* . . .
SOFIA *pulls herself closer.*
She leans down as . . .)
SOFIA: (*Whispers*) Let me tell you. Let me tell you who he is.
ISABELLE *is still for a moment, then, troubled and self-consciously, looks up at* . . .
SISTER CELESTINE, *who is watching her.*
She pauses, then returns to SOFIA.)

INT. CONVENT COURTYARD. A LITTLE LATER.

THOMAS *and* EDWARD *sit and stare at one another.*
THOMAS *takes a cup of tea and moves towards* EDWARD, *offering it to him.*
EDWARD *presses himself back against the wall.*
THOMAS *stops, nods apologetically, and steps back.*
SISTER CELLESTINE *comes walking down the hall and into the courtyard.*
THOMAS: (*Stands*) How is she?
CELESTINE: The bullet shattered her shoulder bone. We can

67

stop the bleeding, but you've got to get her to a hospital.

(*Of* EDWARD . . .) Now what's *his* problem?

(THOMAS *looks back at* EDWARD *and shrugs.*

They watch EDWARD *a few moments longer, then . . .*)

CELESTINE: The girl wants to talk to you.

(THOMAS *turns and looks at her, apprehensive, then follows her out.*)

INT. INFIRMARY. MOMENTS LATER.

THOMAS *has to lean down over* SOFIA *as she works to raise her voice to a mild whisper.*

SOFIA: I told her. I told Isabelle.

(*He leans back up and closes his eyes, wishing she hadn't done this.*)

I told her everything. I told her who you are. I can't forgive you. I can only forget. And I don't want to.

(*And that seems to be about all she has strength to say. She breathes deeply and closes her eyes.*

He watches her drift off to sleep, then just sits back and stares off at nothing for a few moments, tired.)

EXT. CONVENT GARDEN. MOMENTS LATER.

THOMAS *finds* ISABELLE *sitting in the doorway that leads out to a garden at the back of the convent. She's been crying and is quite beaten up by what she has heard.*

THOMAS *touches her shoulder. She just looks at it.*

He hesitates, hurt, then takes his hand away. He says nothing for a moment, then turns and takes a step away. Finally . . .

THOMAS: I'm sorry.

ISABELLE: What are you sorry for? Do you know?

(*He takes this like a punch in the stomach. He almost becomes angry, but then just walks away and sits in a doorway somewhere else in the garden.*)

THOMAS: No. I don't. I don't know what I'm sorry for. But I am sorry. That's got to mean something, right? I mean, whatever it is she told you . . . Whatever it is I was . . . This is me. Now. What else can I do?

(ISABELLE *blinks and glances aside. Then asks . . .*)

ISABELLE: Will you still make love to me?
> (*He pauses a moment, then comes back over to her.*
> EDWARD *is asleep on his bench in the courtyard.*
> THOMAS *touches* ISABELLE's *chin and raises her up to himself.*
> SOFIA *is asleep in the infirmary.*
> THOMAS *and* ISABELLE *kiss.*
> *Afterwards, he leans back to look her in the eye.*)

THOMAS: Eventually.
> (*She smiles.*
> *He breathes easier, then steps back.*)

THOMAS: I'll go pull up the car.
> (*He turns to go, but . . .*)

ISABELLE: Wait.
> (*She removes the gun from her bag.*)
> (*She catches up with him as he walks away.*)
> Here. Take the gun.
> (*He circles her, pausing, then . . .*)
> I've put the bullets back in.
> (*He looks from the gun to her, smiles, then kisses her once again and walks out of the garden and into the convent.*
> ISABELLE *watches him go, feeling better. She pulls back her hair and relaxes. But then . . .*
> *She hears a scrape and looks off to her left.*)

69

A sharp-shooter cop, about twenty feet away, spies into the garden and continues on his way.
ISABELLE *falls back, realizing that everything is wrong . . .*
THOMAS *strides up the large hall towards the front doors . . .*
ISABELLE *comes running through the convent . . .*
THOMAS *moves closer and closer to the front doors . . .*
ISABELLE *is running through the halls . . .*
THOMAS, *gun in hand, pulls back the bolt from the huge front door and looks back over his shoulder as he hears . . .*
ISABELLE *calling as she runs . . .)*

ISABELLE: Thomas!!!!!
(He stops, looking back down the hall over his shoulder, as the huge doors swing slowly open, revealing behind him . . .
An ocean of flashing lights over an army of police cars and cops poised to shoot.
And ISABELLE *comes closer, but . . .*
As the doors roll steadily back, THOMAS *whips back around with his gun drawn to see the cops and . . .*
A policeman fires.
THOMAS *is hit squarely in the heart and thrown to the ground.*
ISABELLE *stops with a gasp.)*

EXT. CONVENT. MOMENTS LATER.

The DETECTIVE *rolls* THOMAS *over. He stands back, confused. A sickening little silence, then . . .*
DETECTIVE: This isn't him.
(The group of cops around him all look at one another, embarrassed and troubled.
ISABELLE *is left alone as she steps up, pauses, then comes down over* THOMAS.
He's dead.
She touches his lips and gazes sadly down at his body.)
DETECTIVE: *(Off)* Miss? *(No response . . .)* Excuse me, miss . . . Do you know this man?
*(*ISABELLE *doesn't respond immediately. She searches* THOMAS's *face and slowly lifts her head and pauses. Then . . .)*
ISABELLE: Yes. *(She looks back down at* THOMAS, *then back up at the cops . . .)* I know this man.

70

Hal Hartley Filmography

As screenwriter/director unless stated:

1984
Kid
Producer: Hal Hartley
Cinematographer (16 mm color): Michael Spiller
Editor: Hal Hartley
Assistant camera and makeup/costume: Carla Gerona
Cast: Ricky Ludwig (*Ned*), Leo Gosse (*Ned's father*), Janine
   Erickson (*accordion girl*), Karen Sillas (*Patsy*), Bob Gosse
   (*Bruce*), George Feaster (*Ivan*), Pamela Stewart (*Ivan's sister*),
   David Troup (*the boyfriend*)
33 mins.

1987
The Cartographer's Girlfriend
Producer: Hal Hartley
Cinematographer (16 mm color): Michael Spiller
Production designer: Carla Gerona
Editor: Hal Hartley
Cast: Marissa Chibas (*girl*), Steven Geiger (*boy*), George Feaster
   (*George*), Lorraine Achee (*Mom*), Robert Richmond (*Dad*),
   Karen Sillas, David Troup, Rick Groel
29 mins.

1988
Dogs
Producer: Hal Hartley
Screenwriters: Hal Hartley, Steven O'Connor, Richard Ludwig
Cinematographer (super-8 color): Steven O'Connor
Art director: Liz Hazan
Cast: Ricky Ludwig, Mike Brady, Gary Sauer
20 mins.

1989
The Unbelievable Truth

Production company: Action Features
Producers: Bruce Weiss, Hal Hartley
Executive producer: Jerome Brownstein
Cinematographer (color): Michael Spiller
Production designer: Carla Gerona
Editor: Hal Hartley
Music: Jim Coleman, Phillip Reed (guitarist), Wild Blue
   Yonder, the Brothers Kendall
Cast: Adrienne Shelly (*Audry Hugo*), Robert Burke (*Josh
   Hutton*), Christopher Cooke (*Vic Hugo*), Julia McNeal
   (*Pearl*), Mark Bailey (*Mike*), Gary Sauer (*Emmet*), Katherine
   Mayfield (*Liz Hugo*), David Healy (*Todd Whitbread*), Matt
   Malloy (*Otis*), Edie Falco (*Jane, the waitress*), Jeff Howard
   (*irate driver*), Kelly Reichardt (*his wife*), Ross Turner (*their
   son*), Paul Schultze (*Bill*), Mike Brady (*Bob*), Bill Sage (*Gus*),
   Tom Thon (*news vendor*), Mary Sue Flynn (*girl at counter*)
90 mins.

1990
Trust
Production company: Zenith Productions Ltd./True Fiction
   Pictures in association with Film Four International
Producer: Bruce Weiss
Executive Producer: Jerome Brownstein
Line Producer: Ted Hope
Cinematographer (color): Michael Spiller
Production designer: Daniel Ouellette
Editor: Nick Gomez
Music: Phillip Reed, the Great Outdoors
Cast: Adrienne Shelly (*Maria Coughlin*), Martin Donovan
   (*Matthew Slaughter*), Rebecca Nelson (*Jean Coughlin*), John
   MacKay (*Jim Slaughter*), Edie Falco (*Peg Coughlin*), Gary
   Sauer (*Anthony*), Matt Malloy (*Ed*), Susanne Costollos
   (*Rachel*), Jeff Howard (*Robert*), Karen Sillas (*Nurse Paine*),
   Tom Thon (*deli man*), M. C. Bailey (*Bruce*), Patricia Sullivan
   (*Ruark boss*), Marko Hunt (*John Coughlin*), John St. James
   (*Mr. Santiago*), Kathryn Mederos (*factory woman*), Bill Sage
   (*John Bill*), Julie Sukman (*biker mom*), Robby Anderson
   (*Joey Blech*), Christopher Cooke (*diner guy*), Bea Delizio
   (*woman on couch*), Tamu Favorite (*salesgirl*), Leo Gosse

(*Uncle Leo*), Elizabeth Gouse (*Grace Blech*), Mildred Jones
(*nurse no. 2*), Pathena Parish (*factory girl*), Scott Robinson
(*bartender*), Nena Segal (*Aunt Fay*), Jean Kay Sifford (*Lori*),
Pamela Stewart (*Mrs. Blech*)

1991
Theory of Achievement
Production company: Yo Productions Ltd. #2/Alive from Off
  Center
Producers: Ted Hope, Larry Meistrich
Cinematography (color): Michael Spiller
Production designer: Steven Rosenzweig
Editor: Hal Hartley
Music: Jeffrey Howard, Ned Rifle, John Stearns
Cast: Bob Gosse, Jessica Sager, Jeffrey Howard, Elina
  Lowensohn, Bill Sage, Naledi Tshazibane, M. C. Bailey,
  Nick Gomez, Ingrid Rudfors
17.45 mins.

Ambition
Production company: Good Machine, Inc., and Twin Cities
  Public Television, Inc./Alive from Off Center
Producers: Ted Hope, James Schamus
Executive producer: Alyce Dissette
Associate producer: Larry Meistrich
Cinematography (color): Michael Spiller
Production designer: Steven Rosenzweig
Editor: Hal Hartley
Music: Ned Rifle
Cast: George Feaster, Patricia Sullivan, Rick Groel, Jim
  McCauley, David Troup, Chris Buck, Margaret Mendelson,
  Julie Sukman, Lasker, Bill Sage, Larry Meistrich, Michael
  McGarry, Casey Finch, Adam Bresnick, Elizabeth Feaster,
  Francie Swift, Lisa Gorlitsky, Mark V. Lake, Bob Gosse,
  Ernesto Gerona, Nancy Kricorian
9 mins.

Surviving Desire
Production company: True Fiction Pictures Ltd./American
  Playhouse

Producer: Ted Hope
Executive producer: Jerome Brownstein
Cinematography (color): Michael Spiller
Production designer: Steven Rosenzweig
Editor: Hal Hartley
Music: Ned Rifle, the Great Outdoors
Cast: Martin Donovan (*Jude*), Mary Ward (*Sofie*), Matt Malloy
(*Henry*), Rebecca Nelson (*Katie*), Julie Sukman (*Jill*),
Thomas J. Edwards, George Feaster, Lisa Gorlitsky, Emily
Kunstler, John MacKay, Jim McCauley, Vinny Rutherford,
Gary Sauer, Steve Schub, Patricia Sullivan, David Troup, the
Great Outdoors (Hub Moore, John Sharples, Dan Castelli,
Craig Adams)
60 mins.

1992
Simple Men
Production company: Zenith Productions Ltd./American
Playhouse Theatrical Films in association with Fine Line
Features, Film Four International, BIM Distribuzione
Producers: Ted Hope, Hal Hartley
Executive producers: Jerome Brownstein, Bruce Weiss
Cinematography (color): Michael Spiller
Production designer: Dan Ouellette
Editor: Steve Hamilton
Music: Ned Rifle
Cast: Robert Burke, (*Bill McCabe*), Bill Sage (*Dennis McCabe*),
Karen Sillas (*Kate*), Elina Lowensohn (*Elina*), Martin
Donovan (*Martin*), M. C. Bailey (*Mike*), Christopher Cooke
(*Vic*), Jeffrey Howard (*Ned Rifle*), Holly Marie Combs (*Kim*),
Joe Stevens (*Jack*), Damian Young (*Sheriff*), Marietta Marich
(*Mom*), John Mackay (*Dad*), Bethany Wright (*Mary*),
Richard Reyes (*security guard*), James Hansen Prince (*Frank*),
Ed Geldart (*cop at desk*), Vivian Lanko (*nun*), Alissa Alban
(*waitress*), Margaret A. Bowman (*Nurse Louise*), Jo Perkins
(*Nurse Otto*), Mary McKenzie (*Vera*), Matt Malloy (*boyish
cop*)
104 mins.

1993
Flirt
Production company: Action Features, Inc.
Producer: Ted Hope
Associate producer: Carleen Hsu
Executive producer: Jerome Brownstein
Cinematography (color): Michael Spiller
Production designer: Steven Rosenzweig
Editor: Steve Hamilton
Music: Ned Rifle, Jeffrey Taylor
Cast: Bill Sage (*Bill*), Parker Posey (*Emily*), Martin Donovan
   (*Walter*), Robert Burke (*Men's Room Man #3*), Karen Silas
   (*Dr Clint*), Hannah Sullivan (*Trish*), Liana Pai (*Phone Booth
   Girl*), Michael Imperioli (*Michael*), Erica Gimpel (*Nurse*),
   Paul Austin (*Men's Room Man #2*), Harold Perrineau (*Men's
   Room Man #1*), Holt McCallany (*Mac the Bartender*), Jose
   Zuniga (*Cab Driver*), Patricia Scanlon (*Woman at Bar*)
24 mins.

The Only Living Boy In New York
(Music Video for Everything But The Girl)
Cinematography (color): Michael Spiller
Editor: Steve Hamilton
4.10 mins.

From A Motel 6
(Music Video for Yo La Tengo)
Cinematography (color): Michael Spiller
Editor: Steve Hamilton
3.00 mins.

Iris
(Video produced for No Alternative Compilation)
Cast: Parker Posey and Sabrina Lloyd
3.50 mins.

1994
Amateur
Production company: UGC in association with American
   Playhouse Theatrical Films and Channel Four Films. A

77

Zenith/True Fiction Pictures Production
Producers: Ted Hope, Hal Hartley
Executive producers: Jerome Brownstein, Scott Meek, Lindsay Law, Yves Marmion
Cinematography (color): Michael Spiller
Production designer: Steve Rosenzweig
Editor: Steven Hamilton
Music: Jeffrey Taylor, Ned Rifle
Cast: Isabelle Huppert (*Isabelle*), Martin Donovan (*Thomas*), Elina Lowensohn (*Sofia*), Damian Young (*Edward*), Chuck Montgomery (*Jan*), David Simonds (*Kurt*), Pamela Stewart (*Officer Melville*), Erica Gimpel (*Irate Woman*), Jan Leslie Harding (*Waitress*), Terry Alexander (*Frank, the Cook*), Holt McCallany (*Usher*), Hugh Palmer (*Warren*), Michael Imperioli (*Doorman at Club*), Angel Caban (*Detective*), Emmanuel Xuereb (*Bartender*), Lennie Loftin (*Taxi Driver*), David Greenspan (*George, the Pornographer*), Adria Tennor (*Kid Reading the* Odyssey), Parker Posey (*Girl Squatter*), Dwight Ewell (*Boy Squatter*), Currie Graham (*Video Store Clerk*), Jamie Harrold (*Pizza Guy*), Patricia Scanlon (*Young Irate Mother*), James McCauley (*Policeman #1*), Benny Nieves (*Policeman #2*), David Troup (*Guard*), Tim Blake Nelson (*Young Detective*), Marissa Copeland (*Sister at Door*), Dael Orlandersmith (*Mother Superior*), Michael Gaston (*Sharp Shooter in Bush*), Paul Schulze (*Cop Who Shoots Thomas*)
100 mins.